TONY TASSET

BETTER ME

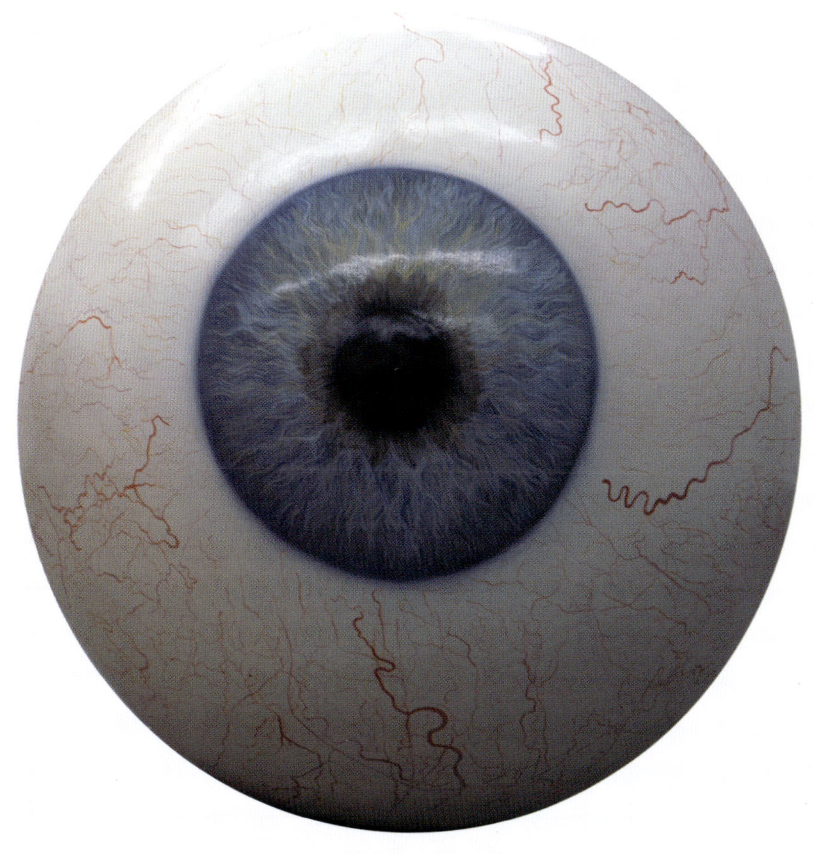

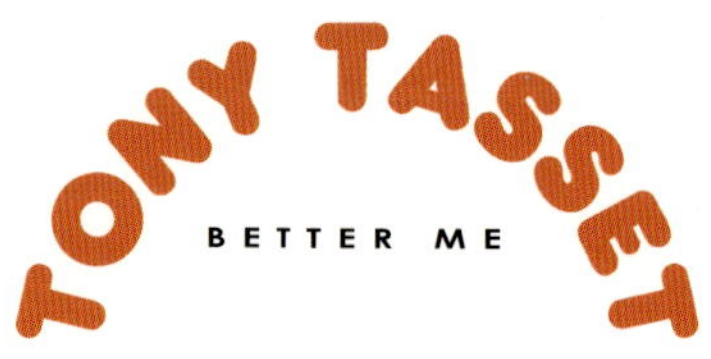

Curated by Barry Blinderman and Bill Conger

© 2003 University Galleries of Illinois State University. All rights reserved.
© 2003 Bill Conger, **STILL LIFE WITH BLUE JAY: ENDGAME IN TONY TASSET'S ART**
© 2003 Barry Blinderman, **WET/DRY: THE TASSET DIMENSION**
© 2003 Michelle Grabner, **ONLY AN EYE, BUT *WHAT* AN EYE**
© 2003 Stuart Horodner, **AN INTERVIEW WITH TONY TASSET**
© 2003 Martin Patrick, **TONY TASSET: THE AMAZING TECHNICOLOR CONCEPTUALIST**
All reproductons of artwork © the artists

Editor: Barry Blinderman
Design: Bill Conger, Barry Blinderman, and Shawn Smith
Production assistance: Angela Barker, Shawn Smith
Publisher: University Galleries of Illinois State University
Printer: Permanent Typesetting and Printing Co., Ltd. Hong Kong
Distributor: Distributed Art Publishers, New York   tel 800.338.2665

Cover: Tony Tasset, **Snowman**, 2003. Photo: John Rizzo

ISBN 0-945558-33-3

This publication has been supported in part by a
grant from the Illinois Arts Council, a state agency.

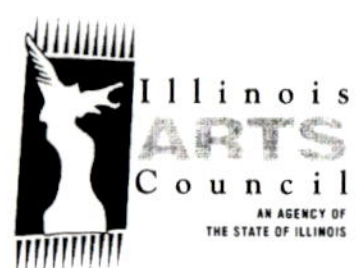

Exhibition dates:

University Galleries of Illinois State University, Normal, Illinois
January 14 - February 23, 2003

Portland Institute for Contemporary Art, Portland, Oregon
March 12 - April 19, 2003

**university
galleries**

Illinois State University
Campus Box 5620
Normal, IL 61790-5620

tel 309.438.5487
fax 309.438.5161
email: gallery@ilstu.edu
www.universitygalleries.com

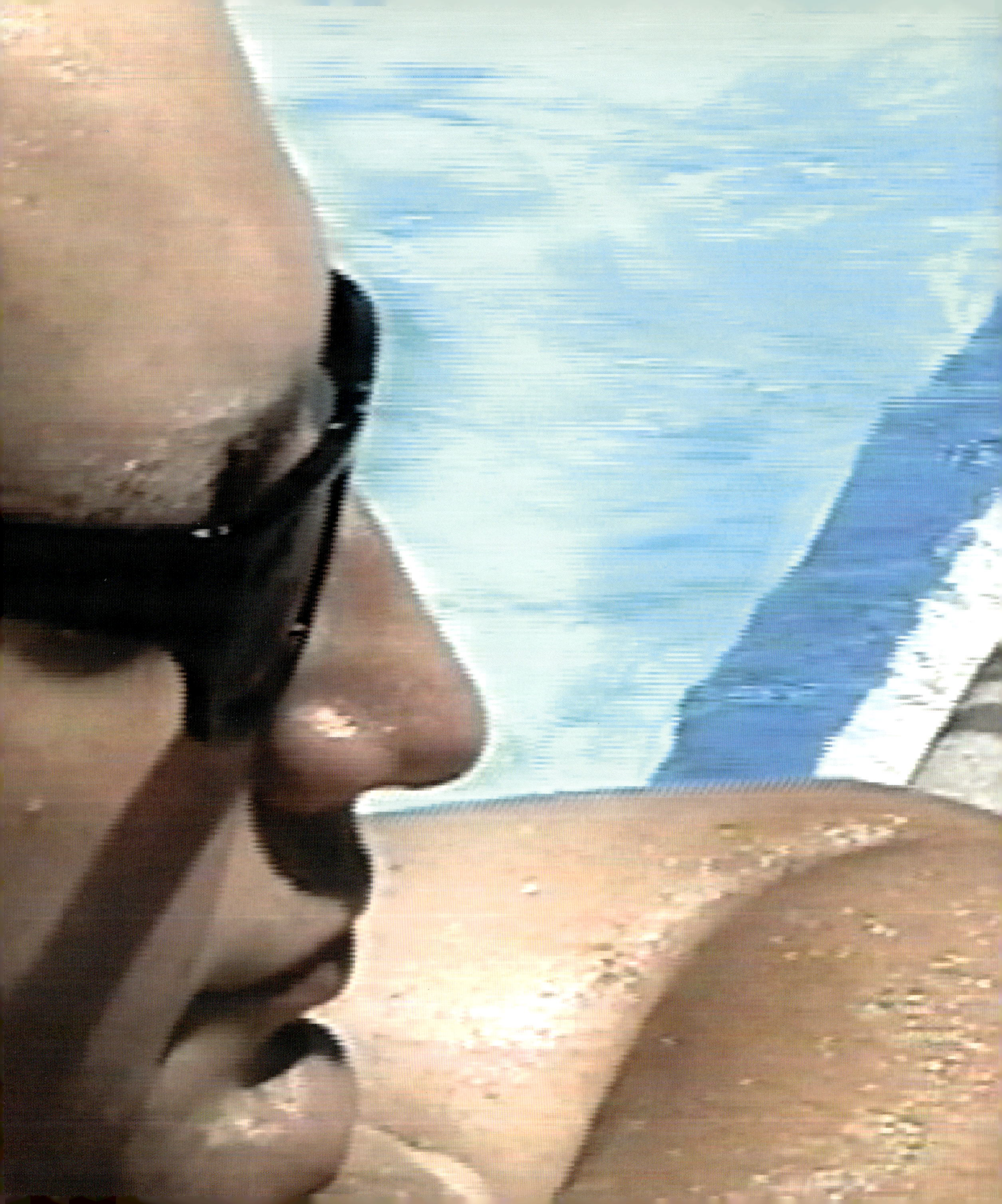

Be regular and ordinary in your life, like a bourgeois, so that you may be violent and original in your work.

—Gustave Flaubert

In the eclectic yet frequently dreary setting of recent art, Tony Tasset is a particularly refreshing presence. He has become increasingly well-known over the past decade through his ongoing efforts to dismantle the newly constructed edifice of "Conceptual Art History" and run wildly around the (de-)construction site. Although Tasset emerged in the late 1980s, and has worked actively since that time, his art remains relatively underexamined by critics.[1] His intriguing and idiosyncratic body of work is also highly diverse in terms of media, from the early sculptures to the more recent photographs, videos, and installations. Tasset often seeks to present a maximum density of content with a minimal amount of "handiwork" (in other words, he skillfully mines the Duchampian tradition), which has probably led him in turn to use photomedia more extensively in recent years.[2]

I have seen Tasset and several of his contemporaries[3] referred to as "neo-conceptualists" but I'm beginning to wonder what that really means, and whether such a term is indeed helpful at all in assessing the scope of this particular artist's production. Maybe it's not a question of *reading* such terms, but of *viewing* his practice. Aren't neo-conceptualists simply younger artists work-

opposite: **In My Room**
DVD   4:48, no sound   2000

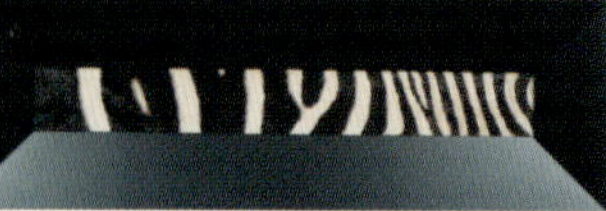

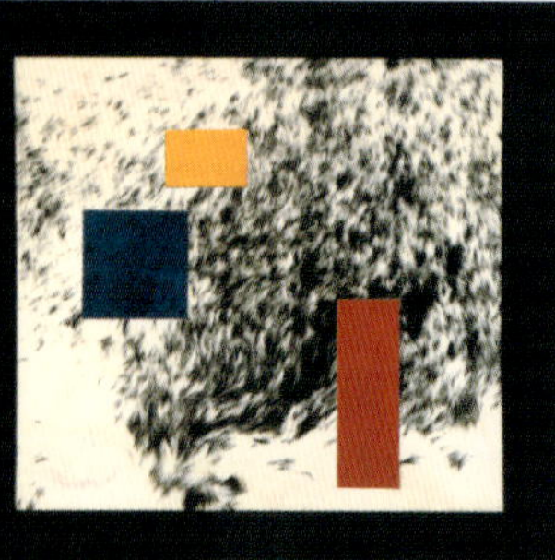

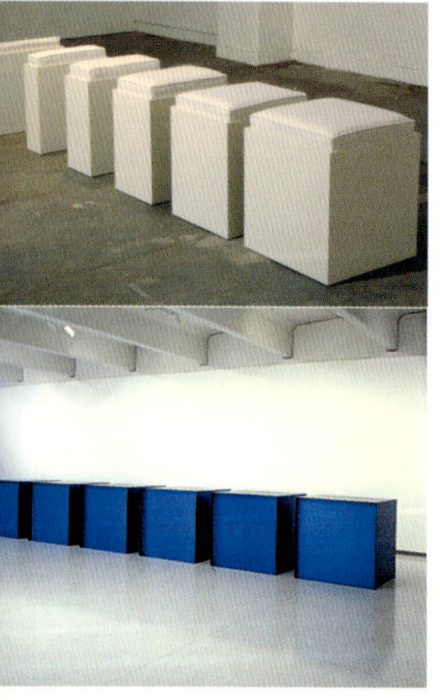

ing in a comparatively recent (and arguably dominant) tradition reaching back to those artists who slouched away from the swollen corpus of high Modernism? Moreover, while it may be useful to at least ponder where Tasset "fits in" in terms of the (neo-) conceptual lineage, it might not do us much good to stick around here too long, in the library, coughing up the dust which has settled upon old art magazines and catalogs.

Nevertheless, several interesting points of reference emerge when considering Tasset's work within a broader art historical framework. Tasset initially exhibited as an artist offering a kind of meta-commentary on previous art movements, particularly both Minimalism and Modernist abstraction. His **Domestic Abstraction** series (1986-87) features framed fur-covered rectangles, representing an unholy marriage between Hans Hofmann and seventies interior design. This was still the era of the long backlash against painting on the part of many artists and critics, and Tasset's work slides comfortably into that discourse. As a matter of fact, a concurrent series was entitled **Comfortable Abstractions**, and integrated leather seat cushions into sculptures akin to Donald Judd's serial plinths and cubes.

Much of Tasset's early work can be understood as an energetic response from a younger artist working in the wake of both Minimalism (Judd, Morris, LeWitt) *and* Post-Minimalism (Hesse, Nauman, Serra). Tasset was building an eloquent infrastructure for his own work largely by referencing the work of others. He proceeded to work his way through Modernist issues related to

Top to bottom: Tony Tasset: Sunshine, 1985; Domestic Abstraction, 1987; Abstract Style;1986. Bench Progression, 1987. Donald Judd, Untitled, 1971.

the legacy of both painted and sculptural form for some time, although aided and abetted by Postmodernist hindsight.

But Tasset's works then became increasingly performative and oriented instead toward the documentation of actions. In the 1993 photograph **Spew**, it's as if Tasset is issuing a look-alike portrayal of Bruce Nauman's 1966 *Fountain*, this time around with blood or pigment—actually chocolate syrup—spurting from the artist's mouth. 1996's video **Squib** portrays Tasset standing against a stark white wall confronting the camera as if transported from a police line-up, and after several seconds of anticipation he is shot—the act is loud, bloody, and startling, but—wait a minute—this is (of course) simply a Hollywood-style stunt. Tasset has flung yet another conceptual boomerang, flying out and sailing back picking up art historical reverberations along the way, such as recalling Chris Burden's infamous 1971 piece *Shoot* in which a friend fired a rifle at his arm. (Significantly in the case of Burden's work, however, real blood was shed, an audience—albeit miniscule—witnessed the act, and the artist staked his claim to a certain kind of macabre notoriety.)[4]

In a work commissioned to accompany a 1995 Robert Smithson exhibition at the Museum of Contemporary Art in Chicago, Tasset played the role of Smithson in order to create a large-scale photographic homage; actually an off-kilter Madame Tussaud's-like rendering, as Tasset/Smithson, with mock seriousness begins to shovel up the desert environs of Las Vegas. We see Mr. Earthworks himself, clad in a straw cowboy hat, hornrim glasses, a garish striped

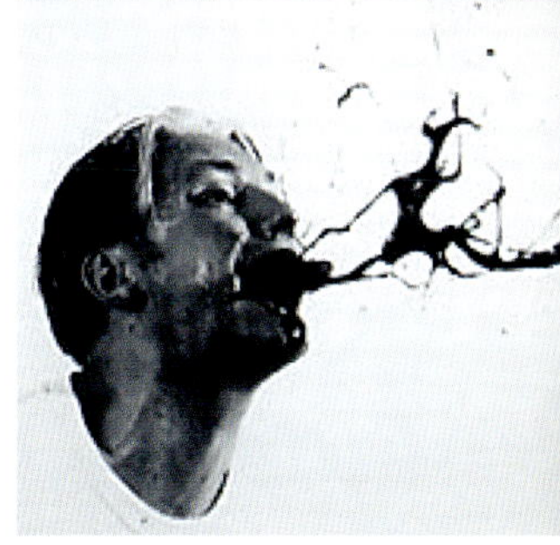

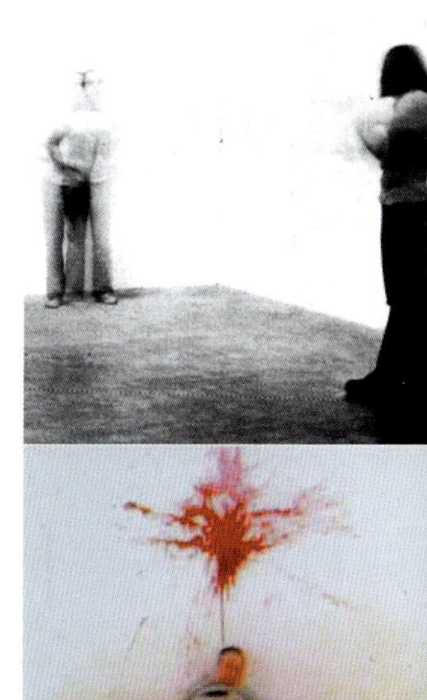

Bruce Nauman, *Self-Portrait as a Fountain*, 1966-70. Tasset, *Spew*, 1993. Chris Burden, *Shoot*, 1971. Tasset, *Squib*, 1996.

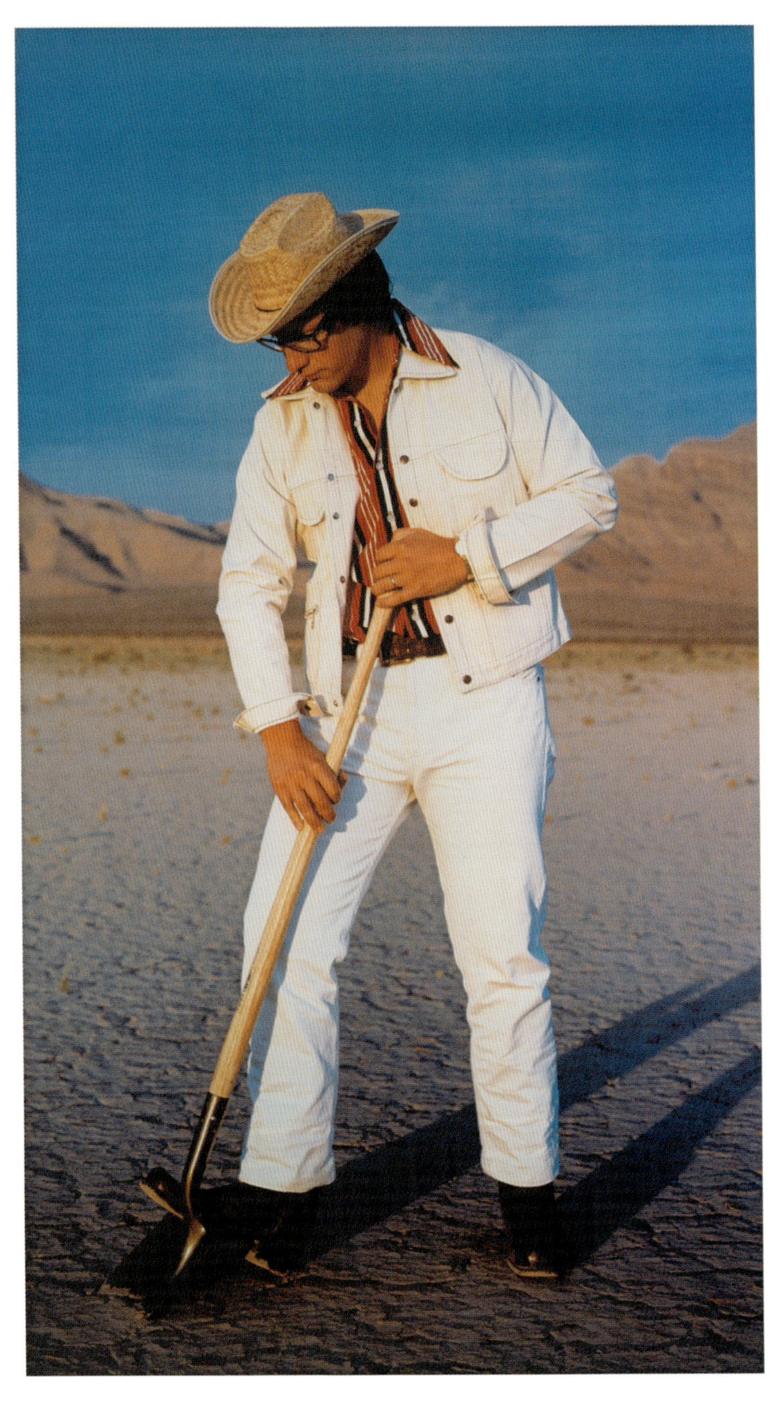

Robert Smithson (Las Vegas)

Cibachrome   83 x 49 inches   1995

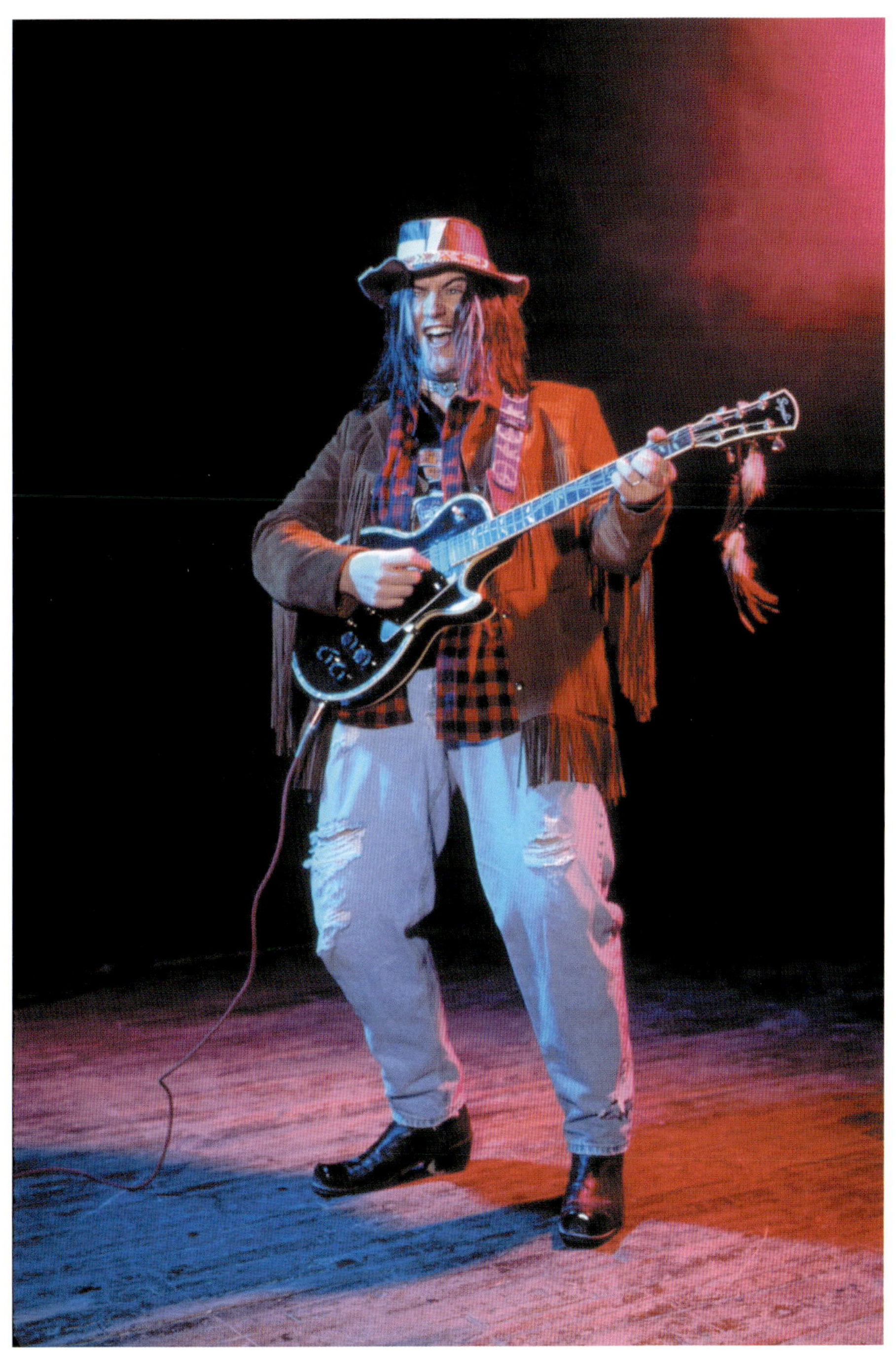

Neil Young

Cibachrome   82 x 48 inches   1997

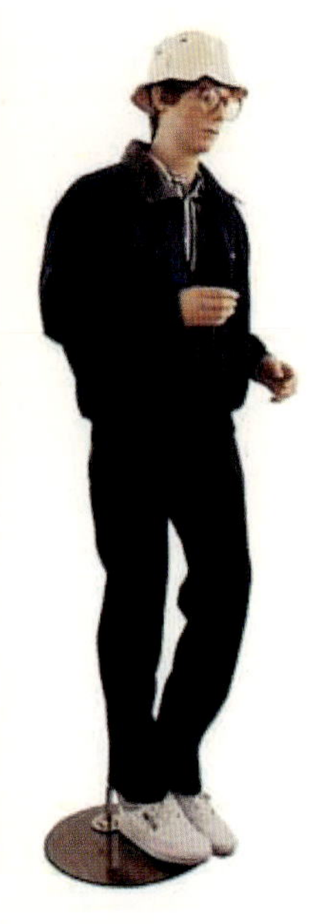

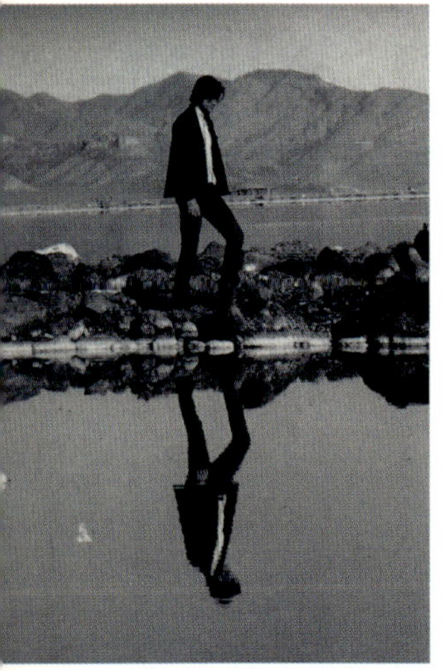

shirt and matching beige Levis and jacket. This is a sixties visionary as depicted by a member of "the Blank Generation" (to use musician and poet Richard Hell's term), a fraudulent image refracted through the looking glass of the Clinton years, a period in which art continued to transform itself into entertainment or seemingly disappear altogether like NEA grants for individual artists or Smithson's own Spiral Jetty, submerged under the Great Salt Lake. [5]

Several artists today are working in territory not unrelated to Tasset's, such as the Italian Maurizio Cattelan, who, with his similar interest in masquerade and madcap humor, has hired a performer to wear a Disneyland-style Picasso costume in the Museum of Modern Art. [6] Other kindred spirits would inevitably include the California-based Mike Kelley, Paul McCarthy, and Charles Ray. All three artists, like Tasset, used their early works to challenge prevailing notions of "standard" art practice: McCarthy made videotapes of himself slithering along his studio floor through wet paint (1972), Kelley fabricated odd plywood birdhouses/geometric sculptures (1978), and Ray emphatically used his own naked body within his quasi-Minimalist sculptures (1981).

Once upon a time they were called "bad boys" (in a ridiculous critical shorthand), but I'm now thinking of some other terms, hmmnn..."nature boy" no, that's not it, yes, it's "suburb boy." Tasset, originally from Cincinnati, Ohio is a blond, forty-something white male who lives in the affluent town of Oak Park, approximately ten miles from Chicago, thus becoming via his demographic profile a truly exotic protagonist for our current narrative. (As with Smithson

Charles Ray, Self-Portrait, 1990. Robert Smithson on the Spiral Jetty, 1970, photo: Gianfranco Gorgoni.

and Kelley, for example, native sons of New Jersey and Michigan, respectively.)

I am charmed and fascinated by Tasset's active incorporation of themes related to rock and roll, which to borrow an old song title, we could call the "sound of the suburbs." [7] The primary example of this approach is Tasset's goofy self-portrait in the guise of Neil Young. I look at this photographic caricature and to me it also resembles some psychotic guitar-wielding version of Ray Bolger's scarecrow from the 1939 *Wizard of Oz* (perhaps America's best contribution to the genre of Surrealist film). Young, who has successfully survived the turbulent events of his generation in both life and art, offers a provocative parallel to the visual artist's own struggle to make work, stay active, and remain visible. As On Kawara's conceptual postcards sent to friends and colleagues in the artworld during the 1970s read, "I am still alive...."

At the end of *my* seventies, I was stuck in a horrible shithole of a private school in the American South. The game of choice among the male students was to induce one another to laugh cruelly at such captivating exhibits on display as: the squirrel-like toupée of the headmaster, the pitifully stuttering farmboy named Jimmy, and the then-handicapped (now mobility-impaired) science teacher. The morning chapel services were the worst, as not only did I have to endure off-key renditions of "Onward Christian Soldiers," but my attempts to suppress laughter were often the most desperate, grueling, and ultimately unsuccessful. At one of these fine occasions, I remember that I couldn't help beginning to urinate, and once it began, I could not stop and piss was running down my leg

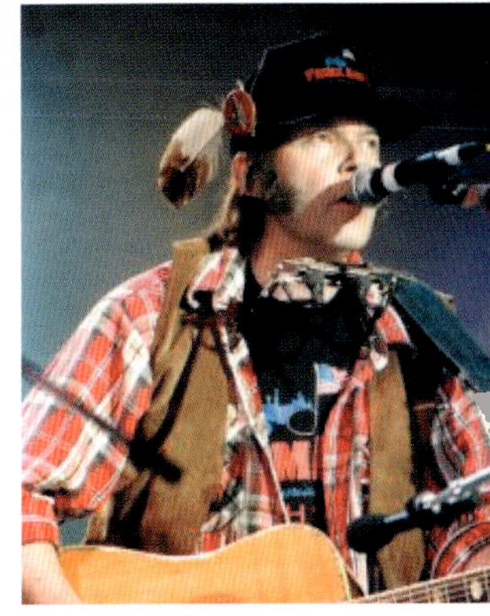

Neil Young. On Kawara, *I am still alive* (detail), 1973.

and my brown polyester pants were getting a nice warm inner coating.

Please excuse the graphic digression above, and I will spare you any further details from my own résumé, but the reason I subjected you to the previous paragraph is that these specific memories "flooded" back to me on seeing Tony Tasset's life-sized self-portrait entitled **I Peed in My Pants** (1994). Arms crossed, the artist looks out at the viewer, his khaki pants recently soaked as well. My willful attempt to digress from my assigned role as art historian and critic just now was an effort to help demonstrate how peculiarly resonant Tasset's meditations on everyday life in the Postmodern world really are. At first glance they might appear seemingly offhand one-liners, but several of Tasset's "comedic" works are actually his most evocative, poignant, and disturbing.

Halloween is the great American holiday as it involves capitalism, spectacle, and cliché in equal measure. Tasset has addressed this yearly event as well in his 1997 **Jack-O'-Lantern**, which is—simply put—a pumpkin with a carved face made of bronze and painted to look like the everyday "real" thing. This exercise in trompe l'oeil again might fall flat if it didn't manage to summon multiple associations from October 31st and its attendant American fantasies and rituals. The most unpleasant neighbors of mine (call them the Smiths, and don't tell them I was talking about them) are fanatically obsessed with decorating for Halloween, traditionally a time when the most uptight suburbanites get to "cut loose." This brings to mind lyrics from the San Francisco punk band the Dead Kennedys' 1982 song "Halloween": *"You'll brag about it for months/Remember*

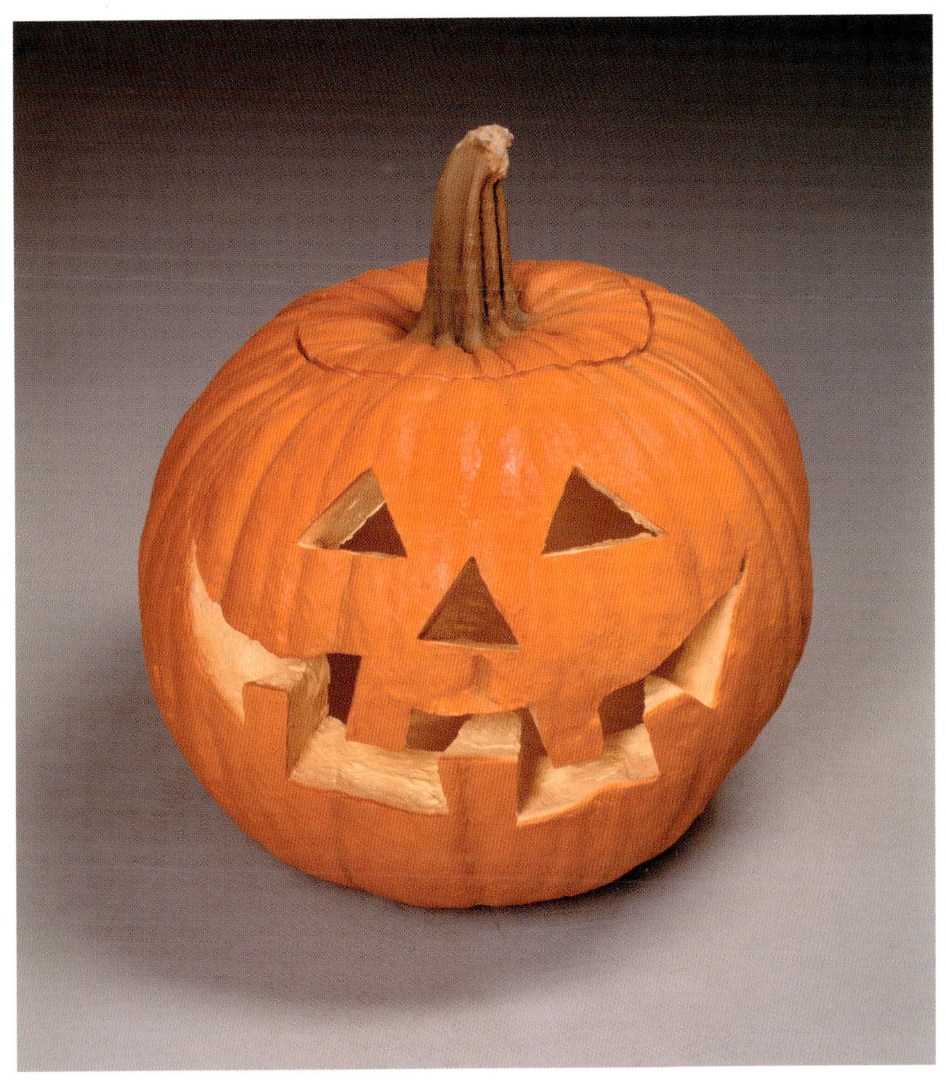

Jack-O'-Lantern,

Oil paint on bronze   15 x 14.5 x 12.25 inches   1997

William J. Hokin Collection, Chicago

what I did/Remember what I was/Back on Halloween/But what's in between/Where are your ideas/You sit around and dream/For next Halloween." [8]

But after all of these accumulated digressions, misreadings, and tirades, I haven't yet talked about some other essential components of Tony Tasset's art, such as his apparent sweetness, calm, and (un-)easy acceptance of the world. (Yes I know I was just quoting Jello Biafra). In contemporary America what truly remains crucial to us after we have left the protective shell of irony, popular culture, and our dubious mythologies behind? I would assert that one's actual experience lived out with family, friends, and lovers then outweighs all else. But how might an artist choose to express and communicate his/her relation to these overwhelmingly significant, but frequently altogether undramatic and visually mundane aspects of life?

In the case of Tasset, he has addressed these concerns by intensively exploring his links with his immediate family and surroundings, and how tenuous, mutable, and fleeting these connections really can be. He has paid homage to his wife, the artist Judy Ledgerwood, in several works, including another large-scale photographic portrait and a 35mm film loop featuring several seconds of Ledgerwood's reaction to the camera's presence. These works take the interrelated notions of "family picture" and "home movie" and import them into the current normative language of contemporary art (the shared field of activity of both Tasset and Ledgerwood, the artist couple): the Cibachrome, glossy and desirable, saturated with brilliant color; and the grandiose conceit of the room-size projection/

installation.[9] However, a loose trilogy of recent film and video works (**Better Me**, 1996; **I Am U R Me**, 1998; and **In My Room**, 2000) seems to offer the most complex portrait of Tasset—and family—so far.

Better Me is a four-segment epic brilliantly laid out in all of six-and-a-half minutes. Here actors fill in for the Tasset family. Of particular note is the artist's "double," a handsome and genial fellow who says all the right things but whose presence almost immediately becomes cloying and unbearable. He is the artist as soap opera hero, nauseatingly nice. We follow him through the following adventures: telling his wife in front of a glowing fire that she needn't work because money's not everything and of course her art is more important;[10] cut to Tasset's twin on the telephone, refusing a retrospective exhibition because his new work is all that counts; segue to Professor Tasset at the University being complimented by a young blond student for changing her life, and finally a gleeful sword fight between "pirate" father and son.

As I mentioned before, the actor-Tasset is numbingly awful to watch, as are the other actors, actually. Do we truly believe such people so familiar to us as types from countless television dramas are somehow our betters, inhabitants of more perfect alternate world where everything's going to be all right? The production standard of **Better Me** is perhaps barely up to the level of a TV movie; thus we are witness to a dreamlike Walter Mitty fantasy voiced in a manner which is simultaneously charmless and professional, generic and frightening. This fantasy of a more perfect life betrays us in all of its imperfect artificial edges.

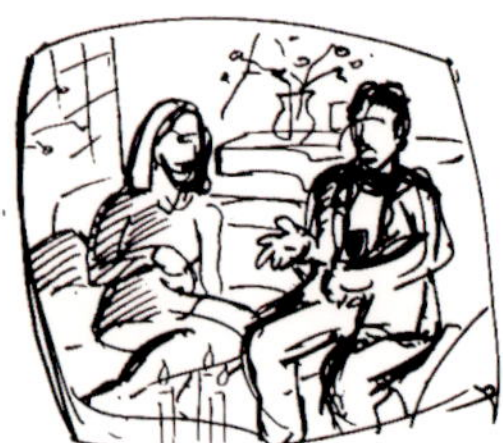

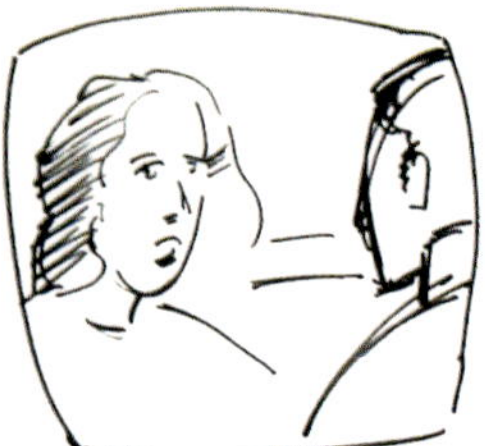

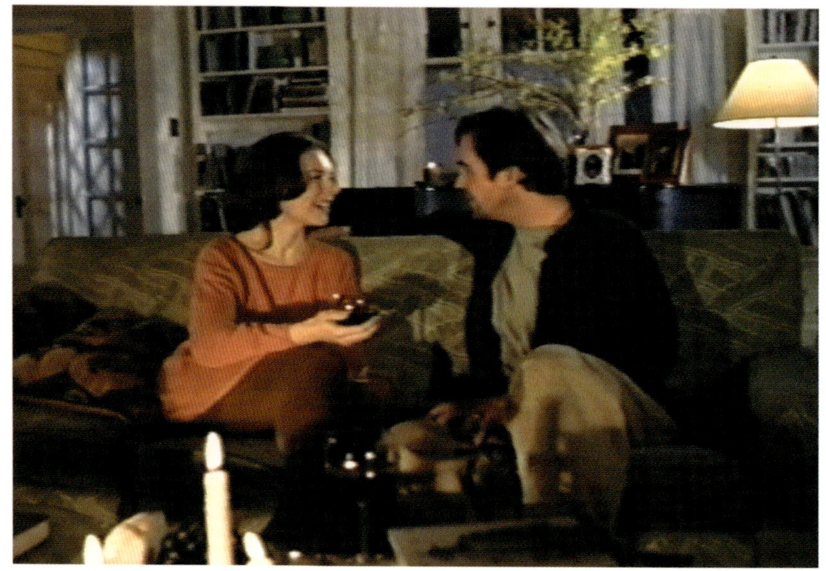

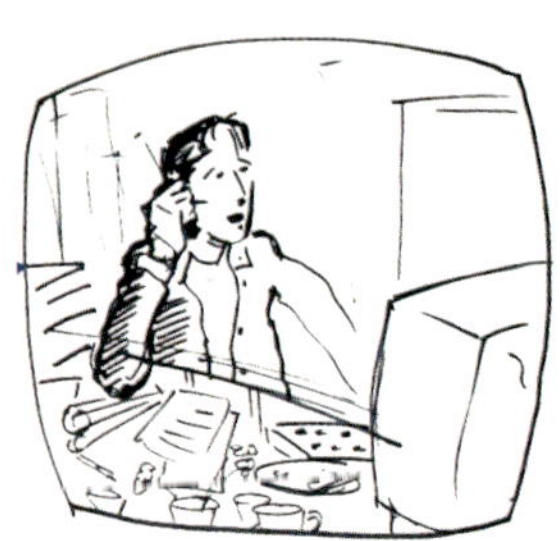

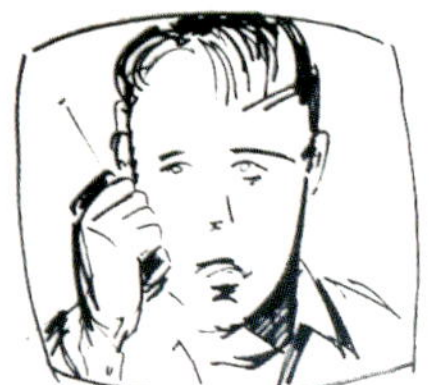

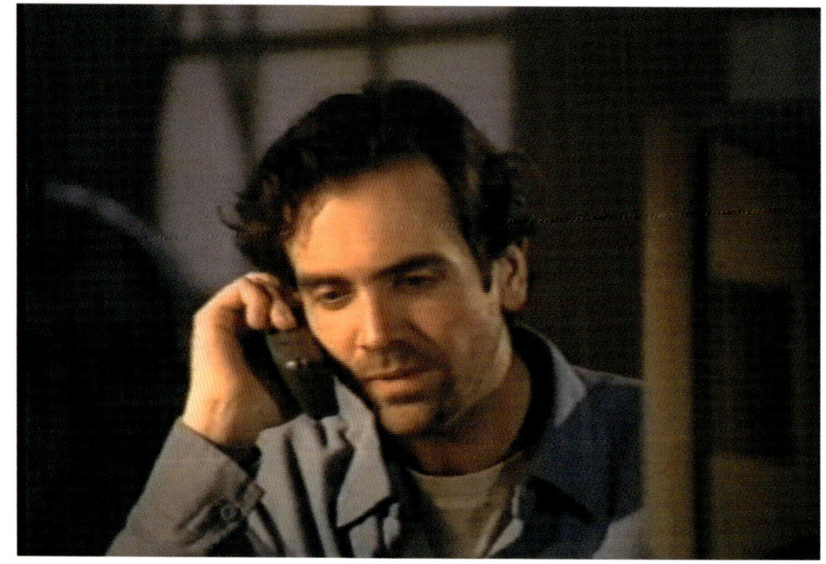

Better Me

DVD   6:30 with stereo sound   1996

Margins: excerpts from the artist's storyboards

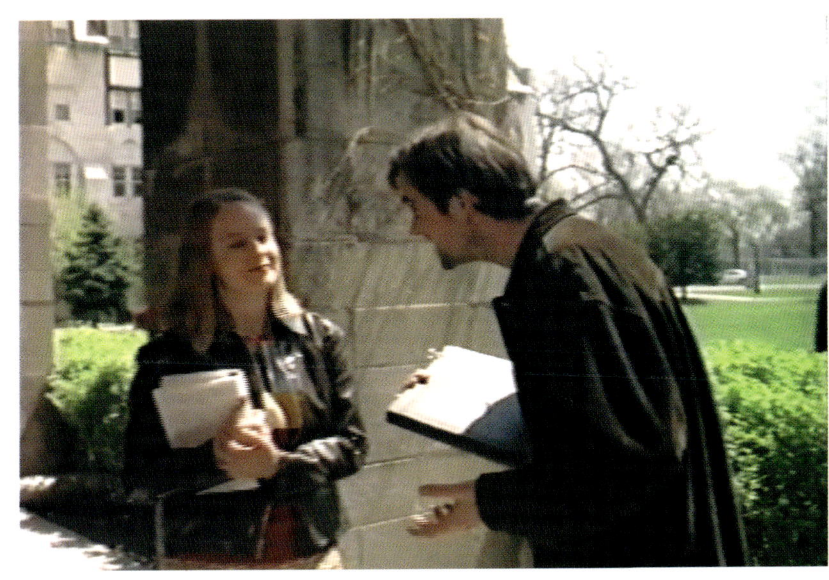

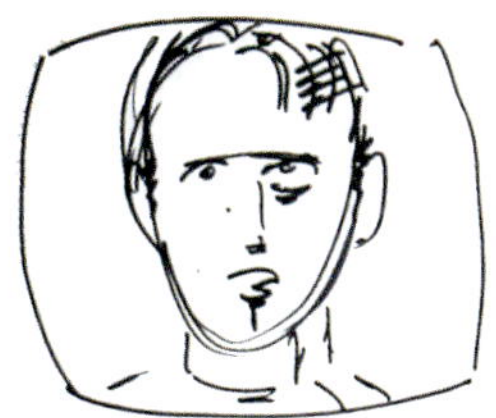

CUT TO: STRAIGHT ON SHOT OF MAN. LOOKING DOWN SLIGHTLY, INTO THE CAMERA

MAN: "I'M HAPPY YOU LIKED THE CLASS, BUT I'M AFRAID YOU MAY HAVE MISSED THE WHOLE POINT. YOU SEE, NOW THAT YOU HAVE GRADUATED I'M SUPPOSED TO REPRESENT WHAT YOU SHOULD WORK AGAINST. I'M THE ESTABLISHMENT, THE OLD GUY, THE GUY YOU'RE SUPPOSED TO HATE."

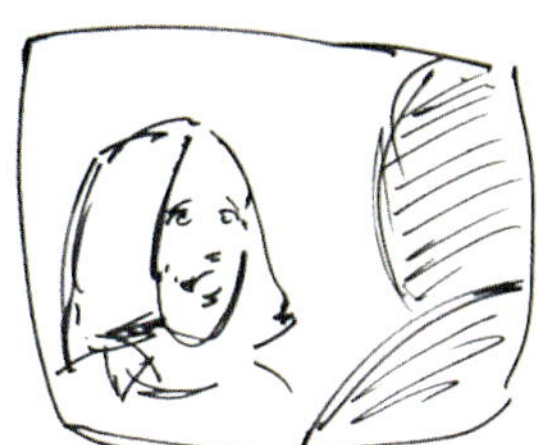

CUT TO: OVER MANS SHOULDER, ¾ VIEW OF STUDENT

STUDENT: "WELL, OK PROFESSOR, BUT I STILL LIKED YOUR CLASS"

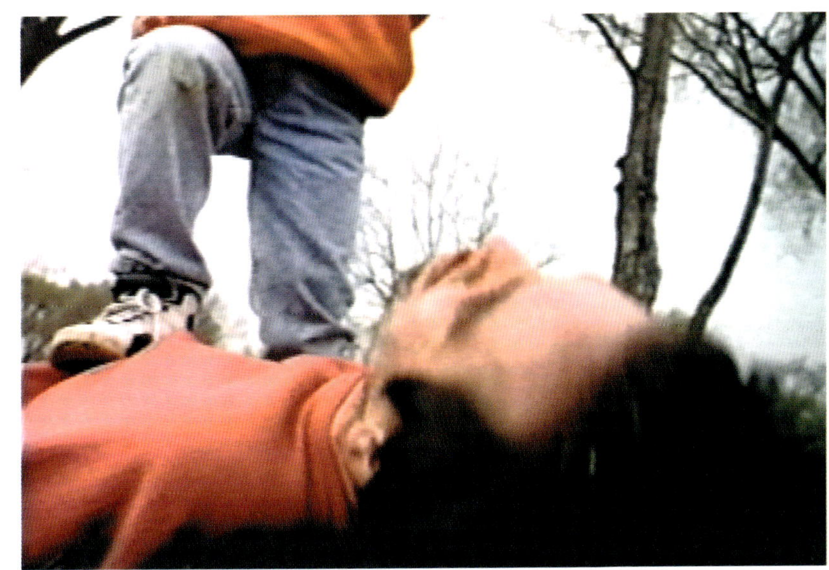

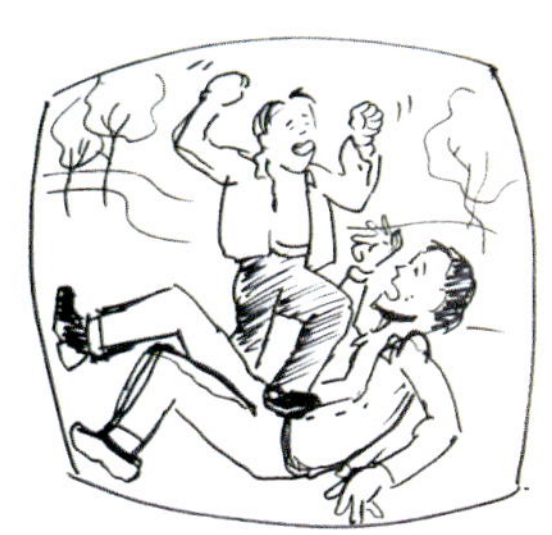

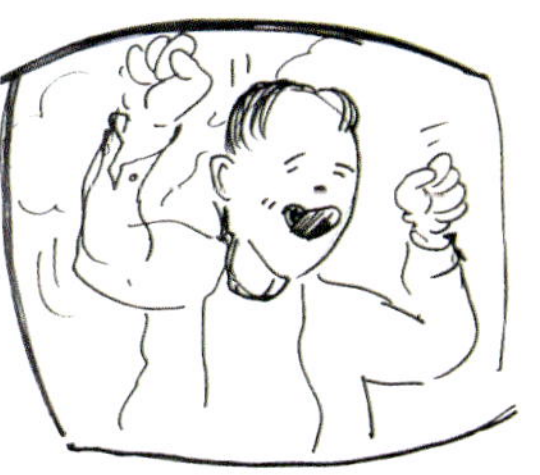

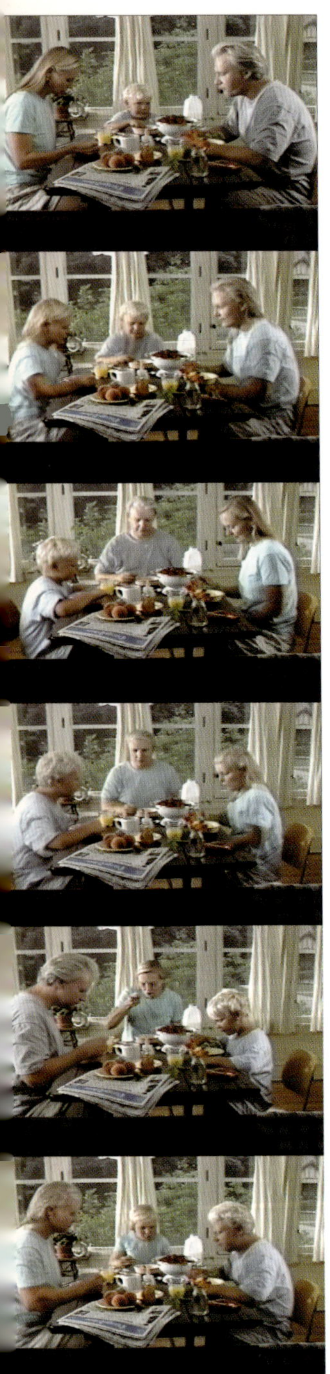

The digitized morphing in **I Am U R Me** is once again a stunt, and not really a new or particularly inspired one at that. Here the cheery (real) Tasset family unit—father, mother, and son—sits eating breakfast around the table; the morning paper is poised on its edge, and a traffic report plays in the background. All of a sudden the likeness of the father is "passed around" the table, as each family member is transformed: father into mother, son into father, mother into son.... If viewed in an MTV video (as once made famous in a Michael Jackson clip) this technique might elicit groans, but in **I Am U R Me** Tasset dares to appropriate stylistic tropes familiar to us from leaden, commercial kitsch and integrate them fully within his work, articulating himself in the crass syntax of our cable television lifestyle. Let's not kid ourselves, he seems to say, if we weren't drinking cheap white wine at a gallery opening we just might be drinking cheap beer at home sprawled in front of the electronic hearth.

The tour de force **In My Room** again summons a reference to popular music, the Beach Boys' song of the same title composed by Brian Wilson, a white suburban male who went to the verge of madness in his life rather than in his art.[11] But there is no musical accompaniment to this video cycle, no soundtrack at all, just a five-minute procession of images— quotidian existence with its "volume" notched up through visual acceleration. **In My Room** isolates Tasset's profile, which occupies roughly half the screen, as he moves through the actions of daily life: talking, eating, sleeping, teaching, kissing, driving, gardening, resting all unfold before us. Only the constant visual anchor of Tasset's ruddy cheek,

Tasset, video stills from I Am U R Me, 1998.

darting eyes, and disheveled hair serves to stabilize this anarchic "day in the life."

In My Room gives us a compressed, framed, boxed-in Tony Tasset. Just as surely as his earlier works take landmarks of Conceptualism, Minimalism, and Performance Art as their points of departure, this video articulates all we in a sense need to and get to know about the artist Tasset himself. At its end, we are suddenly left perhaps wondering, bewildered, or dizzy, but with the clear impression that Tasset has created in the kaleidoscopic breadth of his art his own distinct space, by virtue of a singular, independent mindset, "in his room," indeed.

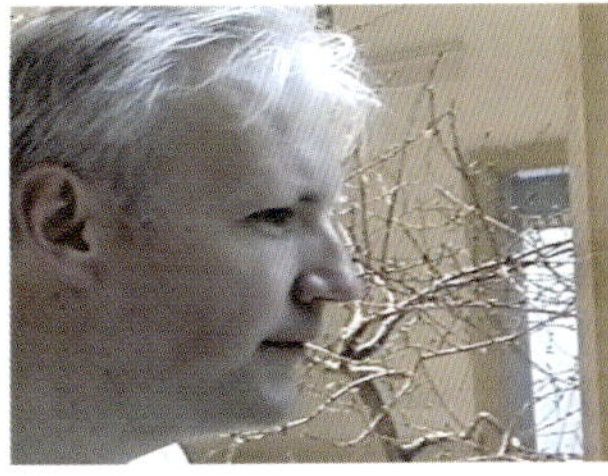
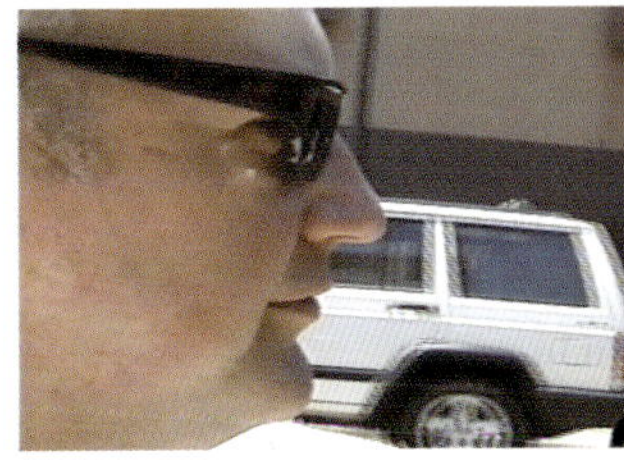
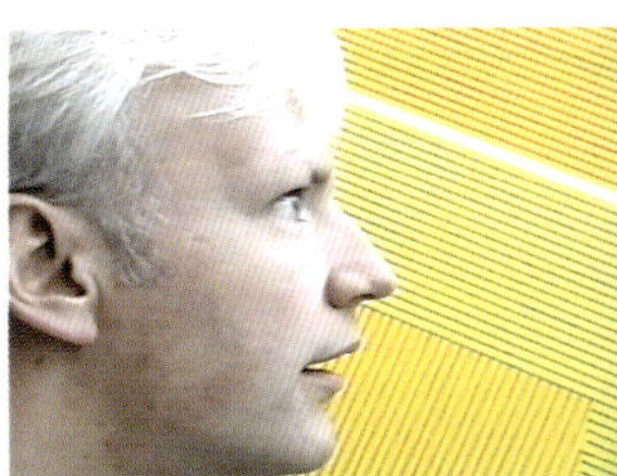
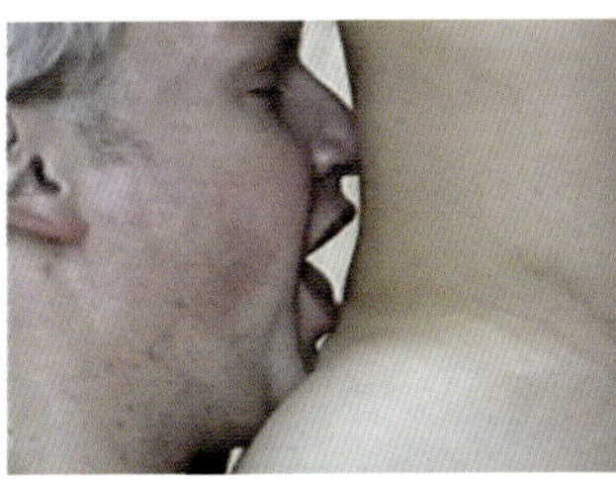
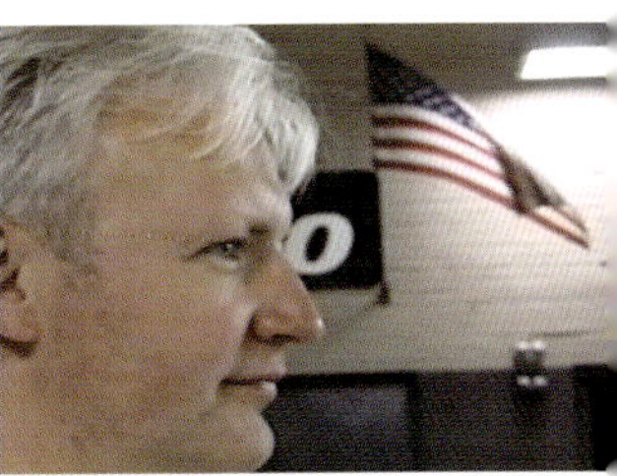
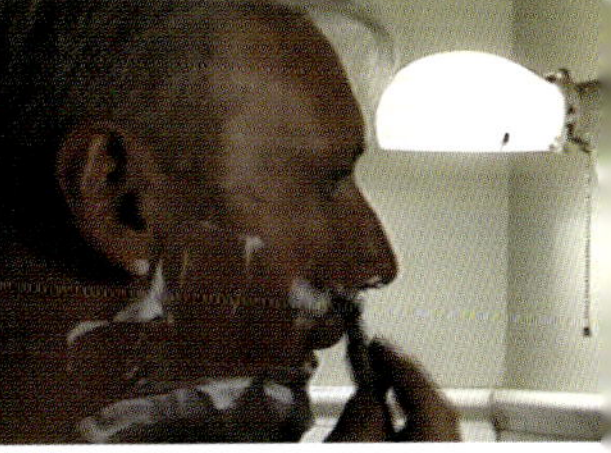

Tasset, video stills from In My Room, 2000.

Endnotes

1. The major exception being a long list of reviews of particular exhibitions, a lengthy profile by Chicago critic Kathryn Hixon ("Transcendence to Transformation: The Art of Tony Tasset" *New Art Examiner*, May 2000) and, interestingly enough, a citation and reproduction of Tasset's 1987 Sculpture Bench in art historian Brandon Taylor's primer on contemporary art, *Avant-Garde and After: Rethinking Art Now* (Abrams, 1995).

2. A remarkable departure from the recent video works is his Cherry Tree (1999), an exacting life-sized sculptural representation of its namesake, created using wax and paint. One might even make the case for a genre of "arboreal" conceptualism, both old and new, with such examples as Michael Craig-Martin's An Oak Tree (1973: "What I've done is change a glass of water into a full-grown oak tree without altering the accidents of the glass of water/The accidents?/Yes. The colour, feel, weight, size..."), Rodney Graham's photographs of trees and camera obscura built to view the image of one in particular, Bluff, Roxy Payne's 50 foot tall stainless steel tree constructed for the 2002 Whitney Biennial and installed in Central Park, and Maurizio Cattelan's placing of an actual olive tree growing out from a large cube of soil in the Manifesta 2 exhibition (Luxemburg, 1998).

3. Jeanne Dunning, Gaylen Gerber, Mitchell Kane, Hirsch Perlman, Joe Scanlan.

4. For more on reactions to Burden's performance, see writer Jan Tumlir's piece in *Artforum* (December 2001) which recalls the work's impact. Here Burden remembers his subsequent encounter with the police: "'I made up some story about a hunting accident and they're going, 'How's your wife?' They were convinced that my wife had shot me. They basically knew there was something fishy going on. . . . To this day people are still pissed off.'"

5. Smithson's earthwork recently (fall 2002) surfaced to modest fanfare, although coincidentally at around the same time *Artforum* published a lengthy tale of one writer's unsuccessful search for the Jetty (Nico Israel, "Non-Site Unseen: How I Spent My Summer Vacation," Sept. 2002).

6. For more on Cattelan's work, see the monograph Maurizio Cattelan (London: Phaidon Press, 2000) with contributions from Francesco Bonami, Nancy Spector, and Barbara Vanderlinden.

7. See UK punk band The Members (1977-1983).

8. From Dead Kennedys, *Plastic Surgery Disasters* LP (Alternative Tentacles Records).

9. For an intriguing examination of artists who have incorporated domestic life into their work, see artist/critic Michelle Grabner's "Test Family: Children in Contemporary Art" *New Art Examiner* (October 1999).

10. I noticed in this scene that on the coffeetable in the foreground lay David Weddle's biography of director Sam Peckinpah entitled *If they move ... Kill 'Em!* (New York: Grove Press, 1994). Peckinpah (1925-1984) was of course the widely acknowledged master of the kind of cinematic bloodletting which Tasset mimics in his own Squib.

11. Although reading the lyrics of *In My Room* (B. Wilson/G. Usher) on the page, it becomes a quite chilling example of white boy alienation: "There's a world where I can go/And tell my secrets to/In my room/In my room (in my room)/In this world I lock out all my/Worries and my fears ... Do my dreaming and my scheming,/Lie awake and pray/Do my crying and my sighing,/Laugh at yesterday/Now it's dark and I'm alone, but/I won't be afraid/In my room ...."

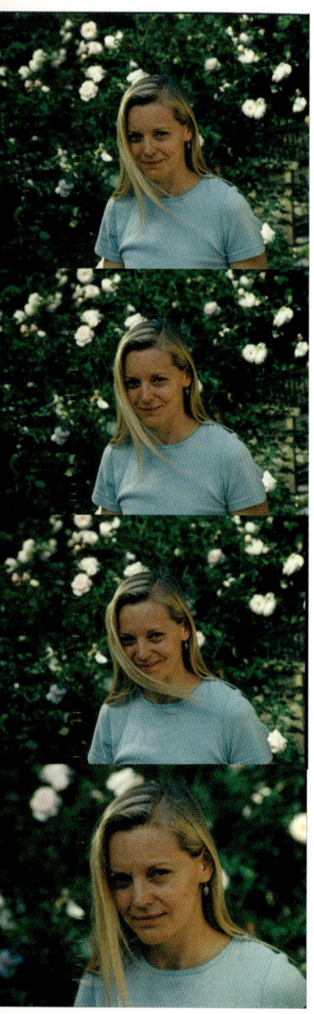

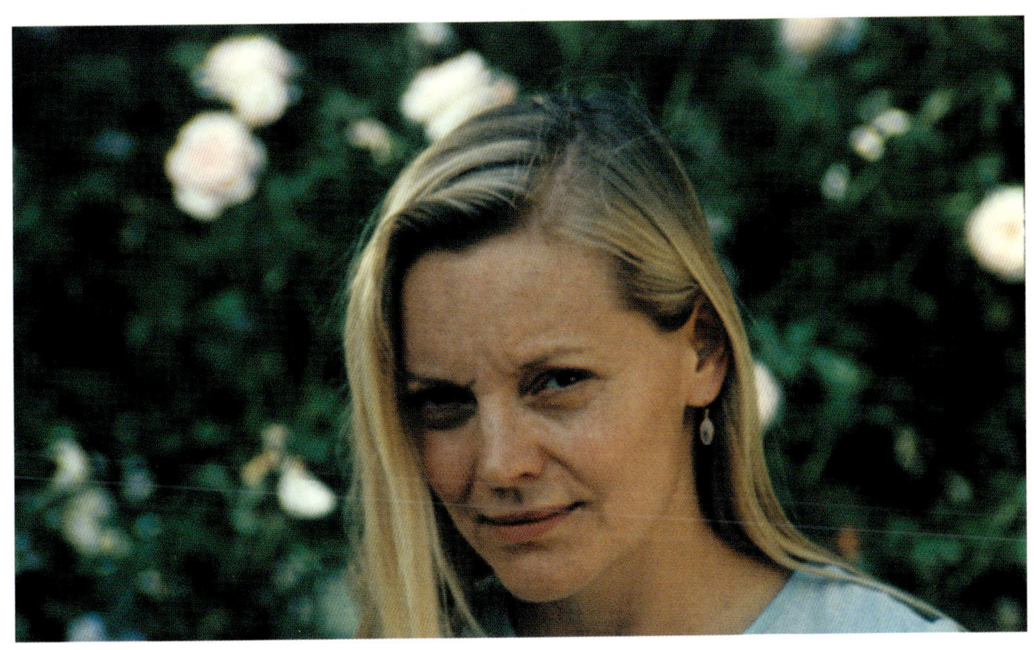

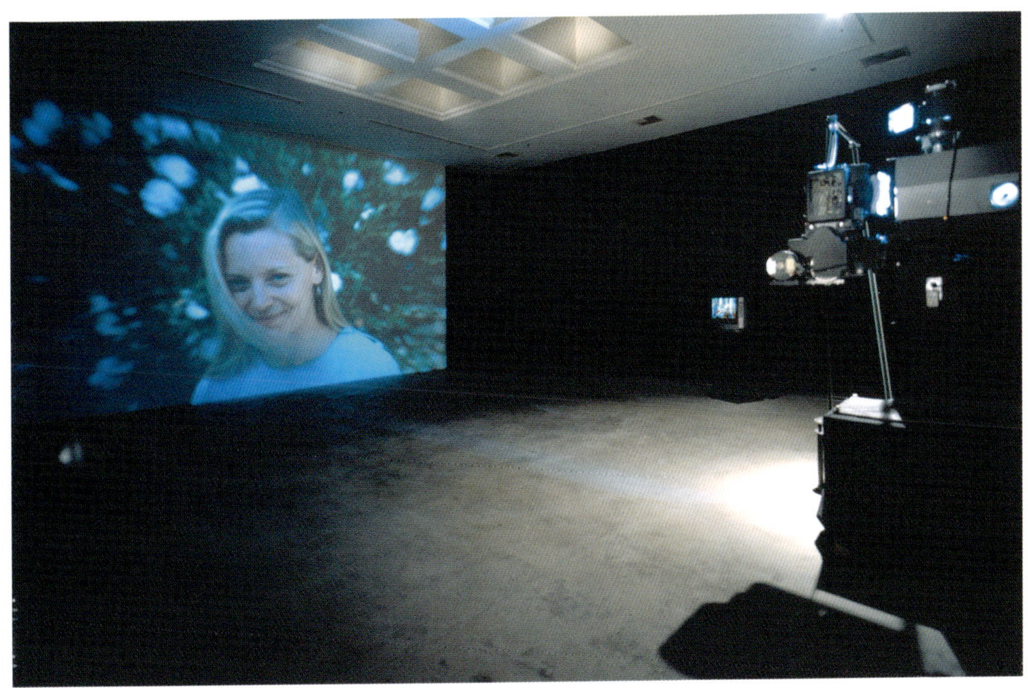

Judy

35 mm projector and :16 film loop, silent   installation at Christopher Grimes Gallery, Santa Monica   1998

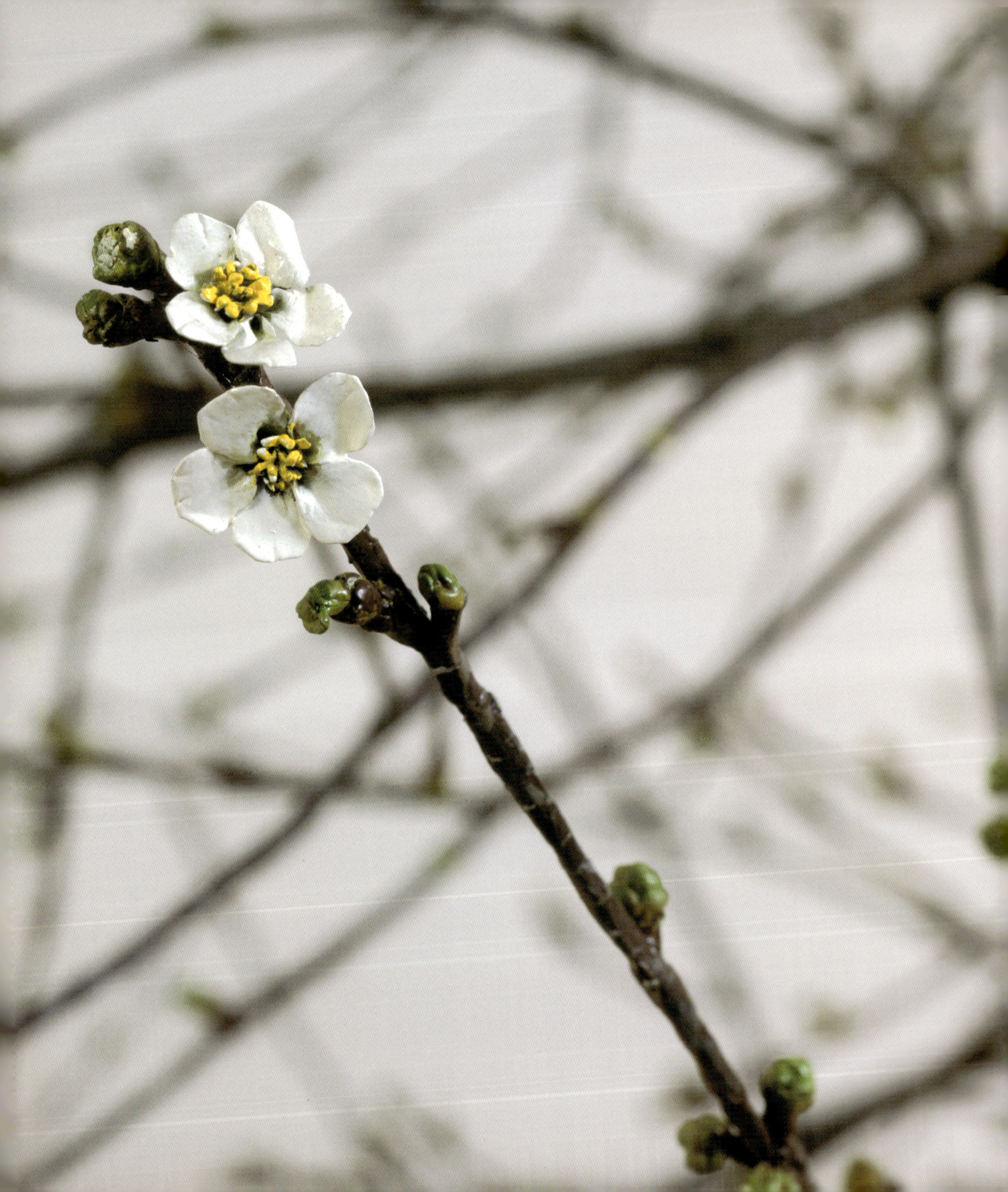

Stuart Horodner: How about "Tony Tasset: This is Your Life" as title for the show?

Tony Tasset: I'm sorry, that's a perfectly reasonable title, but it makes me cringe. After a hard look at this show, I swear I am not going to use myself or my family in any more work! I figure if I quit now the work might have a chance of retaining some dignity. There's a fine line between making art about narcissism and just being narcissistic. But before we get too far I want to know what you get out of the work. Why would anyone care about my life? I portray myself as quite content. I am a middle-class to upper-middle-class white guy, totally privileged.

I don't care about your life (OK, I do), I care about your ideas and objects and how they force me to think and feel. No different than Frida Kahlo self-portraits, or a Richard Serra sculptural space, or a Ray Johnson collage. You're on a road of inquiry that I get to follow—daily rituals, domestic situations, and doubts, desires, vanity, time. Your cherry tree *is not only a lovingly sculpted surrogate, but it's also about the first moment of blossoming, an awakening. And maybe a reminder of the apocryphal story about George Washington with his little hatchet?*

Many people consider me the Frida Kahlo of the Midwest. I am thrilled that you see so many references in my work. I hope to identify the epic, the universal, the poignant, from a very local place—namely my life. We have a small backyard, and

Opposite: Cherry Tree (detail), 1999.

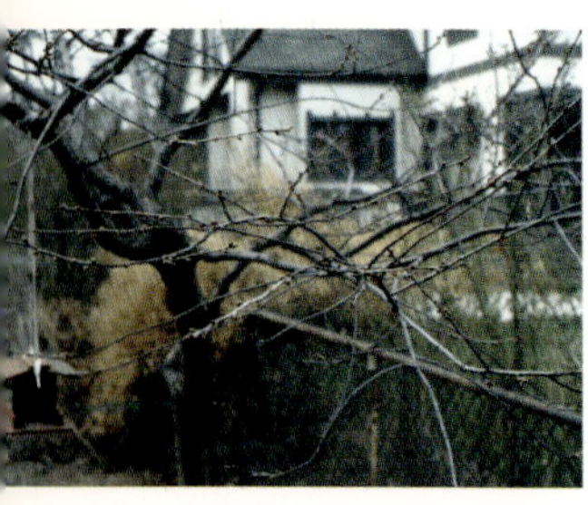

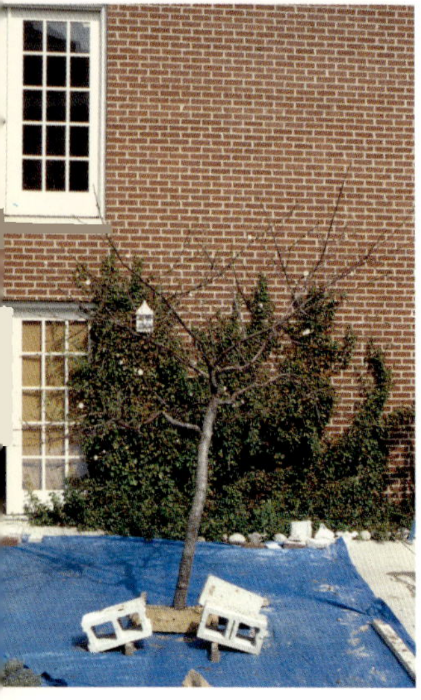

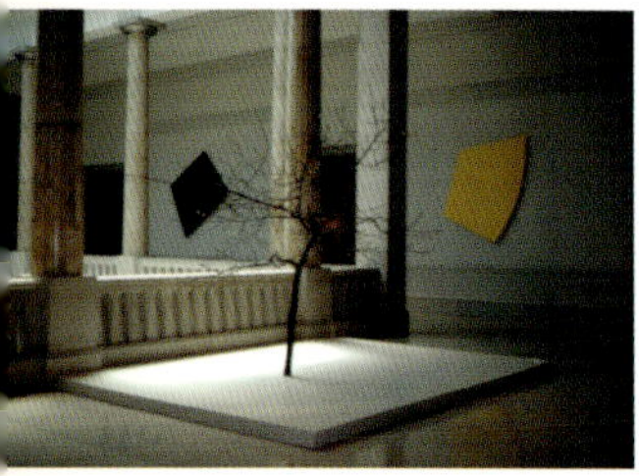

the cherry tree is the only tree in it. When that clumsy little tree first blossoms, it is a moment of heartbreaking beauty that I experience every spring in my real life.

Over the last ten years my work has gotten more personal in content and more populist in aesthetic. When I was 22 all my friends were 22-year old artists and I loved the elitism of our shared passion. At 42 I have a more diverse group of friends with varying degrees of tolerance for the games of contemporary art. I now want to make work that speaks to a wider constituency.

*****Cherry Tree*** captures a moment of "becoming," and I am interested in what you learned by sculpting a copy of a tree in the digital age. Hand forming wrinkled boughs and branches and painting small buds and blossoms. And then there is the **Dead Blue Jay**, a heartbreaking finality. Coming upon it on the gallery floor, there is such displacement, and compressed sadness. What dictated your choices of fabrication?*

In **Cherry Tree** I was trying to get back to making art the way I did as a child. I wanted to re-experience the sheer thrill of copy. I was trying to project wonderment, beauty and hope—"becoming" as you call it. I think I was doing penance for **Squib**. I knew labor equals love to a wide audience. I have no problem giving people what they want. The piece was also just a challenge. It was the old standoff between the artist and nature. I wanted to make the most difficult sculpture I could think of, and it was definitely a humbling experience. I learned that I never wanted to do that again.

Top to bottom: the cherry tree growing in Tasset's backyard. Cherry Tree in production. Cherry Tree installed at the Art Institute of Chicago, 2000.

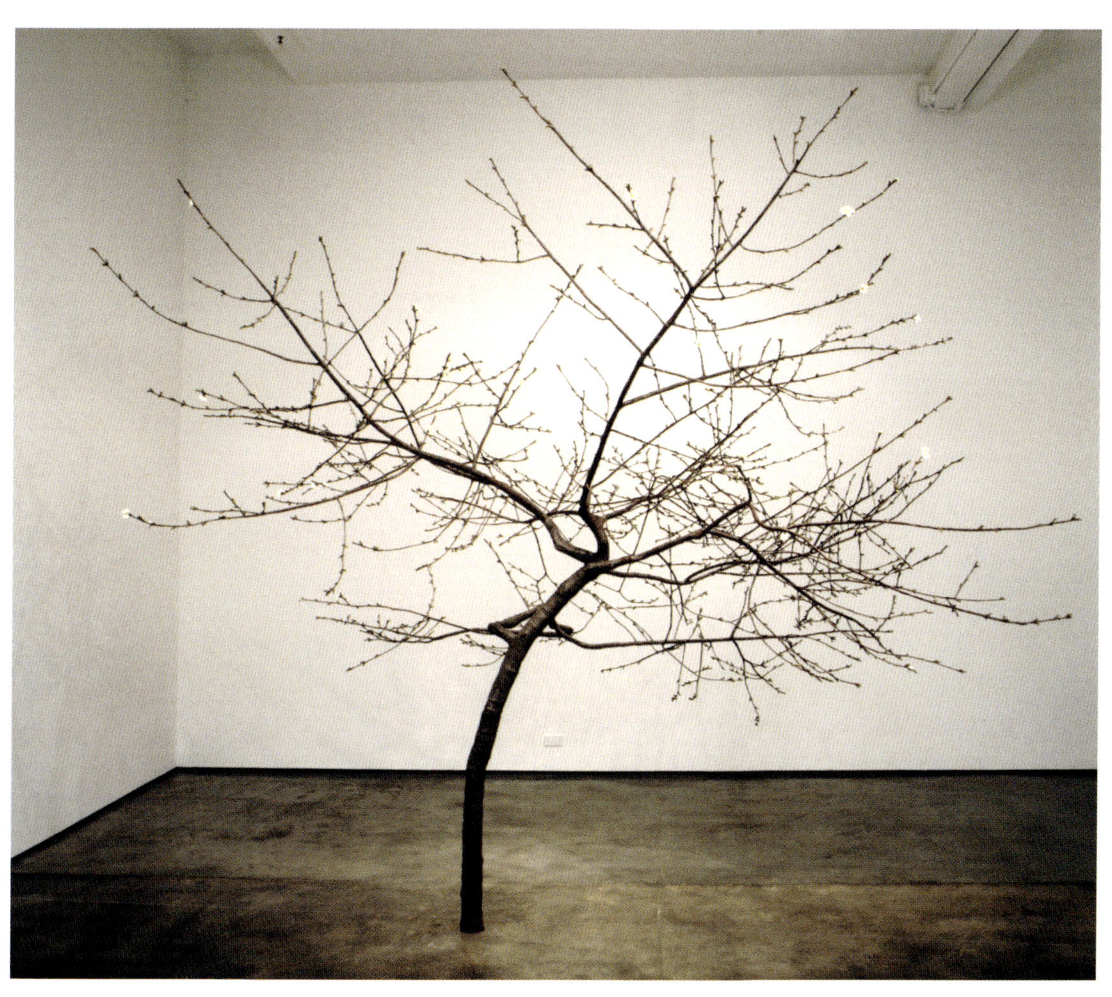

Cherry Tree

Oil paint, wax, and steel armature   120 x 144 x 144 inches   1999

"Nature can kick art's ass," but your tree holds up. Cezanne said "One minute in the life of the world is going by. Paint it as it is." You sculpted that minute.

That's a good quote. With the dead blue jay, I felt if I was attempting to speak about life then I had to take a crack at death. But how could I speak of death without being melodramatic or presumptuous? The blue jay provided an elegant solution. The bird was embalmed, so to speak, and presented directly on the floor. My intention was to view death as directly as possible, without opinion. Also you wouldn't have the visceral reaction—sadness or disgust—to a replicated bird, no matter how good the reproduction. By the way, no bird was killed in the making of my art. I had the idea for that work for several years. One day I arrived home to find the bird in a little baggy on my front porch, with a note from my friend Kevin, who had found it dead in his backyard. When some situations occur it's as if the work just makes itself. Killing a bird or a tree in order to make this work just wasn't the karma I was going for.

The bird has a wide range of life and art issues for me. Of course there is the emotional response, that feeling in the stomach. And the need to bend down and examine it, to look hard at death. But also the history of restoration and preservation, the special aesthetic and scientific skills involved. You're one kind of artist, the taxidermy person another.

That's a scary thought. I wish you had met this taxidermist. But you're right, I often

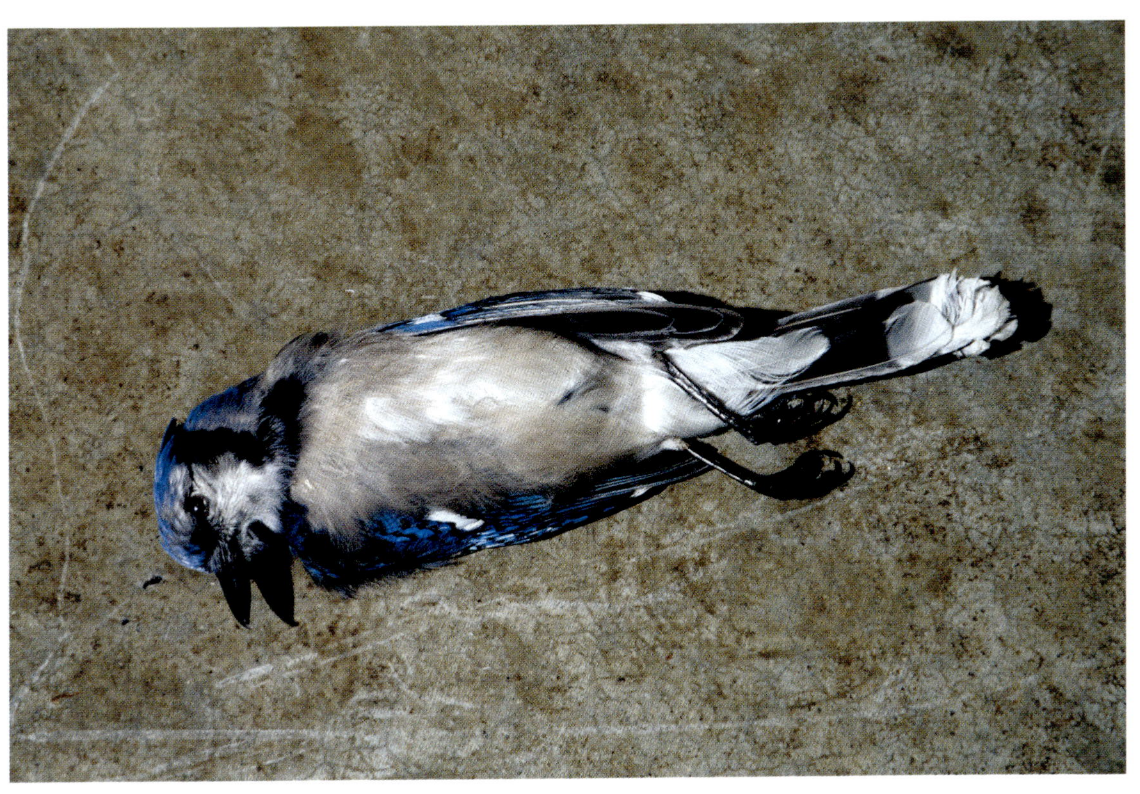

Dead Blue Jay

Taxidermied blue jay   2 x 2.5 x 9 inches   1999

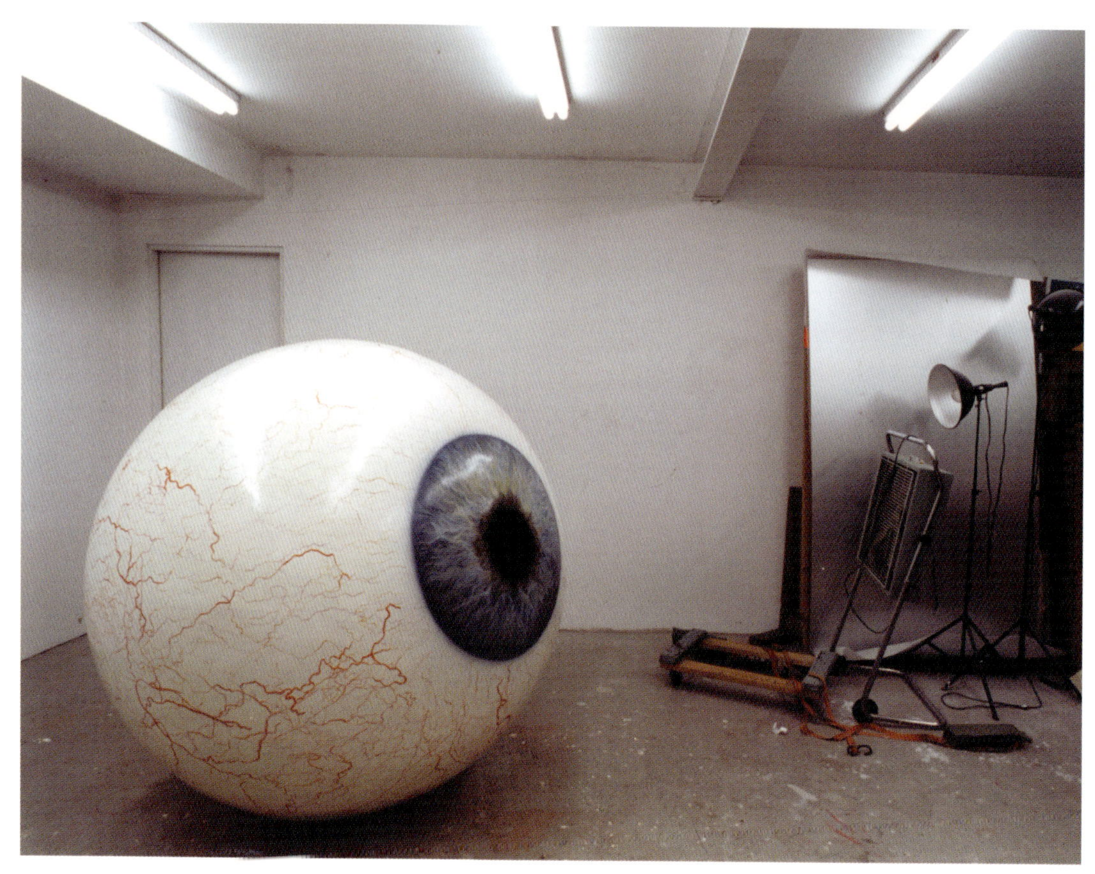

Big Eye

Polystyrene, latex cement, and acrylic paint, 60-inch spheroid, studio view, 2001

use some debased, unconsidered or common sculptural practice for my own means. Did you happen to see my big eyeball sculpture?

I saw the big eyeball and, of course, it saw me. Like the tree, it's a very handmade object compared to your often cooler fabrications—very vulnerable with its tiny blood vessels and milky surface skin. I enjoyed thinking of it in the context of Guston's late paintings of eyeballs roaming the landscape, and Gogol's story "The Nose" and Philip Roth's The Breast. *Body fragments that become whole figures.*

I think I got a little carried away painting those blood vessels. Day after day I would go to my studio, blast Coltrane, paint veins, glaze over them and paint them again. Being in my tiny studio and facing that eye—my eye—*was* very much like being trapped in a Guston painting. I created a monster, an idol of my self-absorption. The slightly crazed experience painting the eye mirrored the neurotic effect I was going for. I don't believe I'm anymore self-absorbed than any other person. (OK, let me think about that). I'm simply using my own experience to try to embody the general state of self-absorption. What finally complicates the issue is that the eye's a very populist piece. It's very rock'n'roll, Ed "Big Daddy" Roth. How many high school textbooks have veiny, bloody eyeballs? It's a classic.

You're the third person who has mentioned Philip Roth's work in relationship to mine. I should send him a catalogue. I do believe narrative is a good way to think of how my works relate to one another, and I often feel that all my work is one big story.

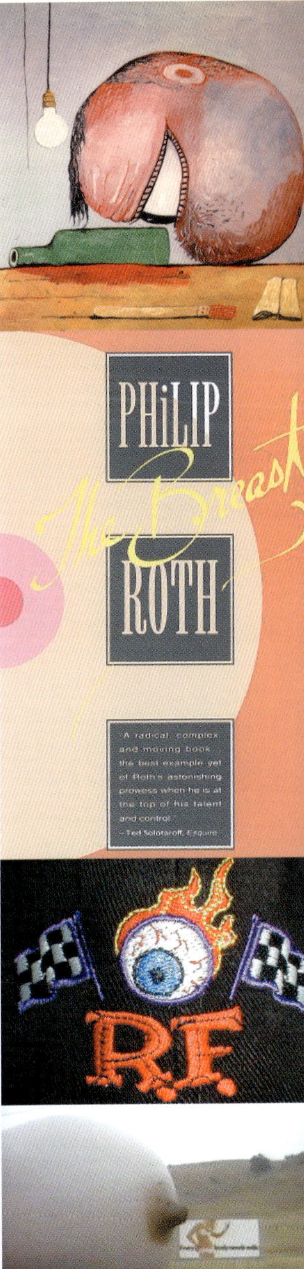

Philip Guston, Head and Bottle, 1975. Book cover, *The Breast.* Embroidered patch based on Ed "Big Daddy" Roth design. Still from Woody Allen's *Everything You've Always Wanted to Know about Sex but Were Afraid to Ask.*

Roth and Guston were friends in Woodstock, New York: Roth escaping the celebrity that followed Portnoy's Complaint *and Guston re-inventing himself as an image maker. They understood each other, and the need for isolation.*

I hate isolation. I wish I was a celebrity.

What was the first art object that you ever made that felt like it was "yours," and why?

The word "yours" makes me a little uncomfortable. I was always apprehensive of the quest for originality. As soon as an artist's "style" can be identified, the artist is doomed. I'm of the "Modernism has failed" generation. My artwork operates more like a theme restaurant: I try to present the quintessential, not the unique.

You've completely done it with **Snowman**. *The three icy snowballs, the carrot nose and branch arms, unwanted leaves and bits of grass—it is just right on. I can feel it in my bones. While honoring a vernacular tradition and the memories of childhood, it also conjures a history of sculpture: forming, carving, adding, the readymade.*

Snowman is brand new. It was conceived of and constructed relatively quickly. As I write this we are in our thirteenth day of war. Even before the war seemed a forgone conclusion, I wanted to take all that smug and stupid American optimism and turn it upside down. I personally feel sad and hopeless—so does my snowman. I hope my snowman affects the way the viewer sees other snowmen in the future.

And maybe how they see men too. Let's talk about the extended self-portrait

Photo-studies for Big Eye.

aspect: your eyeball, your parents, your wife Judy and son Henry, your garden, your day-to-day movements.

Beginning perhaps with **Spew** I started to think that art, at its basis, is an expression of ego, a simple holler: "I exist!" The art object gives the self form. Classic conceptual art taught me to be skeptical of the institution. In the past I had made work about the collector, the gallery, the museum. At some point I asked myself "why am I making art about 'them' and not about me"?

We all live in our own little kingdoms of desire, fear, consumption and delusion. I thought maybe if I got intimate or honest enough in my work, I could find some shared humanity with my audience. At some point, I began to view my life—my existence—as material I could manipulate like clay. It was also a very efficient way to make art. Multi-tasking. I could make art while living my life. A couple of books that influenced the work were *Life the Movie* by Neal Gabler and *Lost Dimensions* by Paul Virilio.

Sometime between **Squib** and **Better Me**, Judy, Henry and I made a commercial for Ameritech. It's a long story. It was interesting being in that situation. They put a ton of money into it and they used Bob Richardson, Oliver Stone's director of photography. It was really over the top. They sort of portrayed our lives, half true and half fabricated. They used our real house and most of our stuff but they also brought in props and gave us a wardrobe. The commercial didn't run very long, but for a month it was all over the place in the Midwest. For several years people both in and out of the art world would recognize me from it and feel

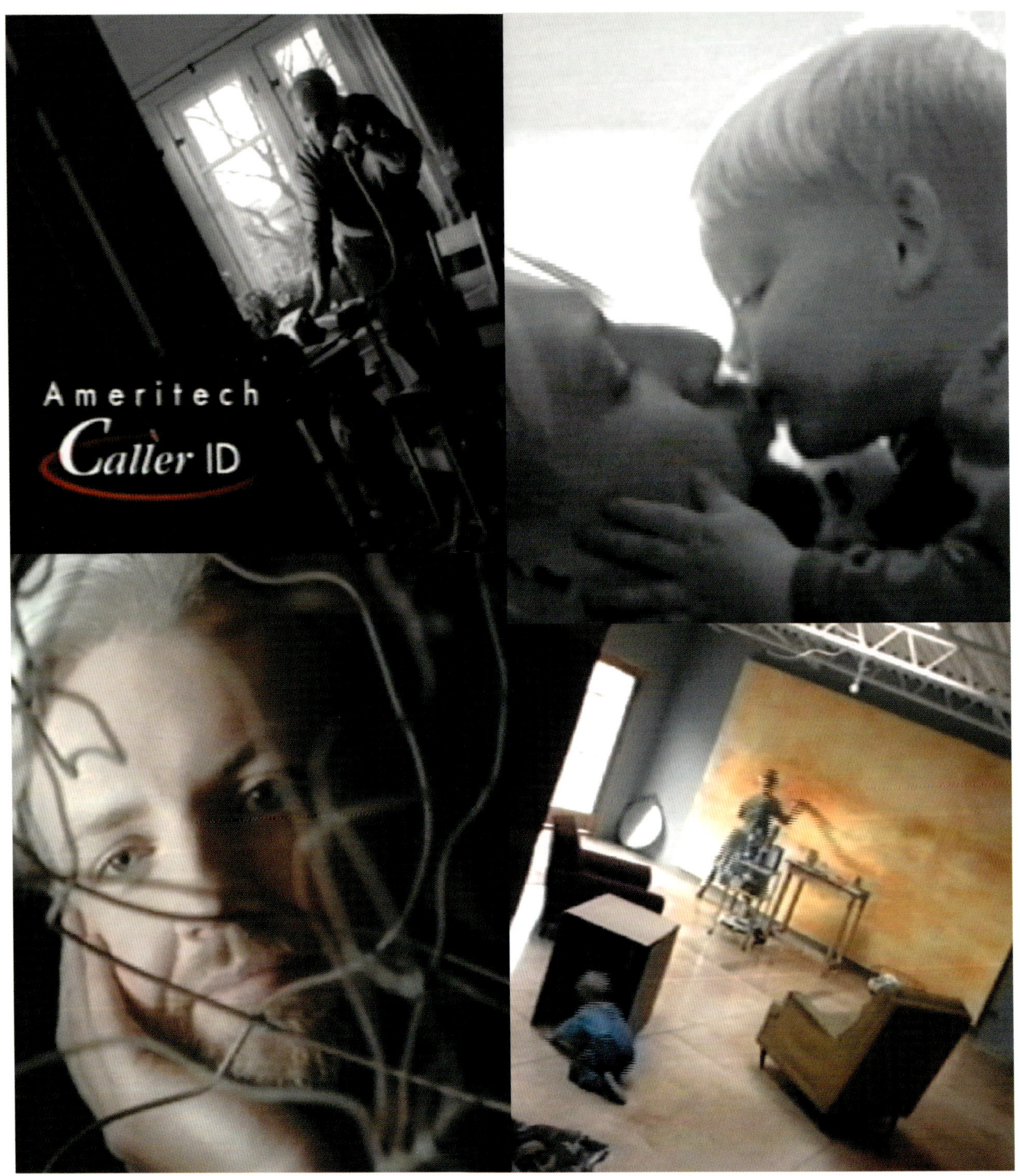
Ameritech
Caller ID

compelled to mention it. That commercial had more effect than my art ever would, which is fine—I understand why: people are more interesting than things. It was a fantastic experience to have my life tweaked, packaged and sold for consumption.

We live in Oak Park and our studios are at our house. Over the years museums have scheduled art tours to the area to see the Frank Lloyd Wright houses, and they sometimes schedule a studio visit with us. Judy teases me because I love to charm these groups of mostly senior citizens into appreciating the humanity and heart of works like **I Peed in My Pants**. I think these groups like to look at how we live more than our art. To see our kid's toys in the backyard. I'm the same way. I like to look at people's houses too.

I am curious about the intersection between the personal and the universal. The photo of Henry's eye is very intimate to me, but at the same time a photo of an eye is the oldest cliché in the book. The viewer can heap a load of interpretation onto it. I like to take signs that are clichéd, that nothing new could possibly be said about, and use them as the starting point. I'm testing the ability to express emotion in a world of signs. Once a curator went on and on to me about how cynical **Cherry Tree** was. I think we've come to a place of such postmodern relativism that we can no longer tell the difference between something that's ironic or sincere. If that's true maybe the artist's role is to once again try to present truth.

Just what is it that makes Judy Ledgerwood so different, so appealing? In your life-size photo of her, she stands near the open window wearing a sexy dress. She has buff arms and strong hands, and there is a curious smile on her face. I've written

Opposite: stills from Ameritech commercial, 1994.

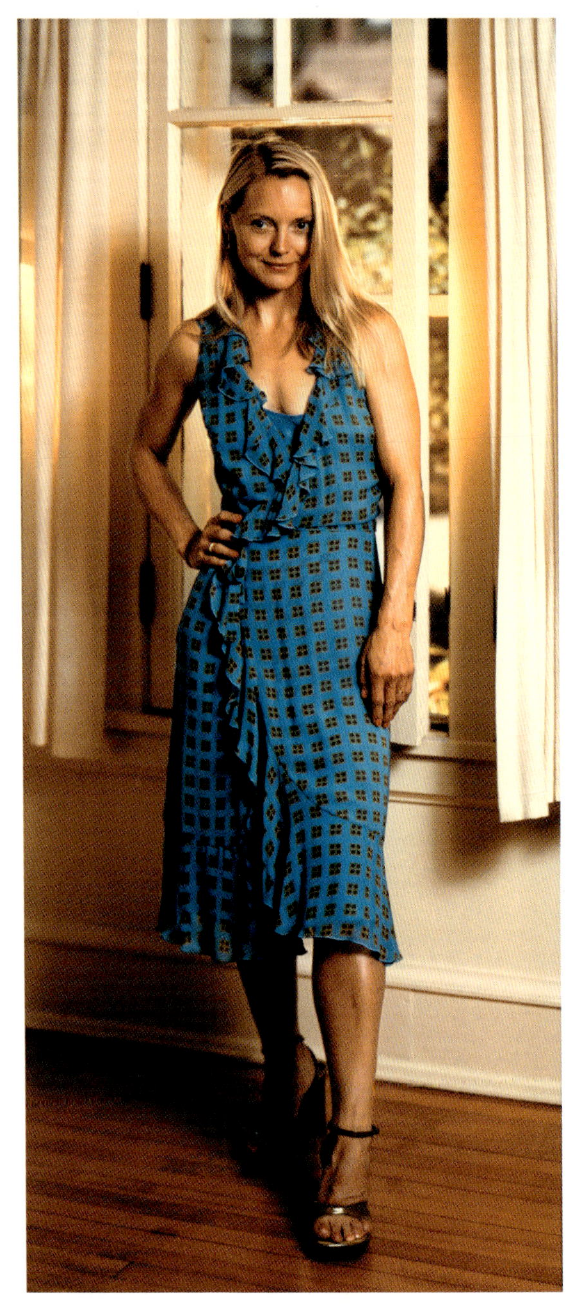

Judy Ledgerwood

Cibachrome   82 x 36 inches   2000

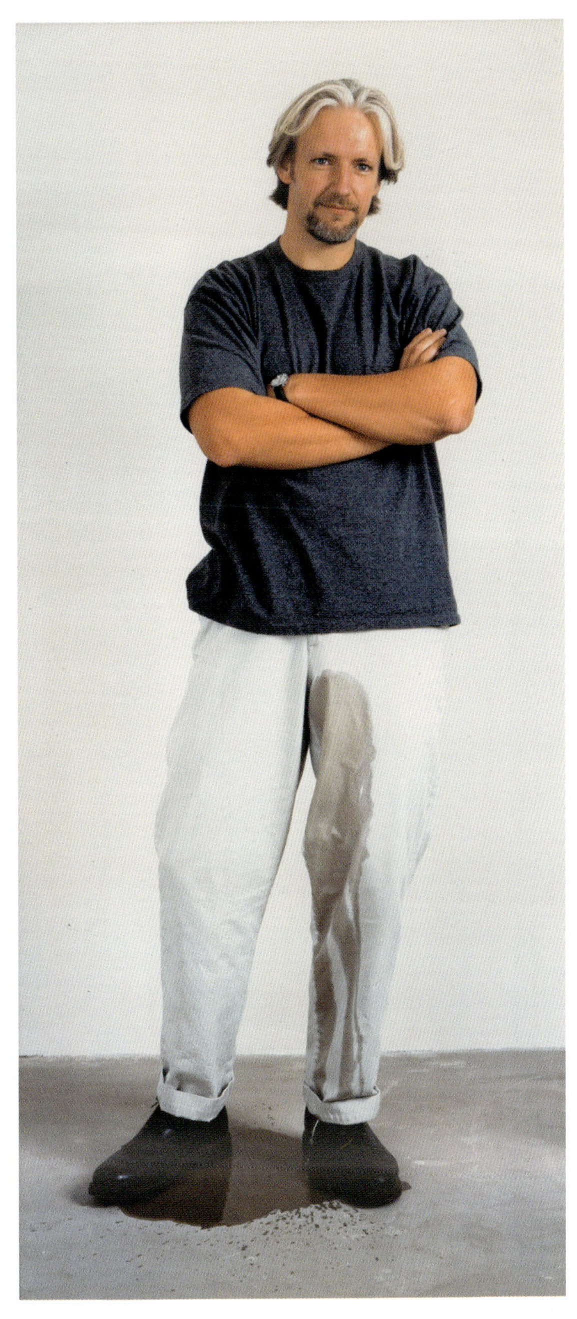

I Peed in My Pants

Cibachrome   83.25 x 38.25 inches   1994

Collection of Refco Group Ltd.

about Judy's paintings but have never met her. By the way, I'm getting married this summer. Any advice?

I never give advice. Yeah, Judy's a babe *and* she's an influence. The works I've made about her are my goddess worship pieces. The photograph **Judy Ledgerwood** was an attempt to restage a moment from real life. One afternoon Judy was getting ready to go out. The sun was going down behind her. Naturally, she looked beautiful. When the actual photo was taken it was high noon. I was on the front lawn angling light from the sun into the window behind her with a mirror and an orange gel. This photo is the same scale as **I Peed**, **Smithson** and **Neil Young**. I wanted to represent her as an influence along with the boys.

I've been thinking about people embodying "place." I live in Portland now, but I think my sensibility is classic New York City.

I've always resisted the idea of regionalism, but you may be right. There is a straight-forward, plain-spoken quality to my work that one could argue is very Midwestern.

What led you to dress up as Robert Smithson and Neil Young? Why did you want to be them for a while?

Because they're Bob and Neil, dude! I'm a shaman evoking spirits, a superfan expressing devotion. Smithson is the great spiritual antidote to Warhol, and Young is the last hippy. Both represent a relationship to the sixties and what that era

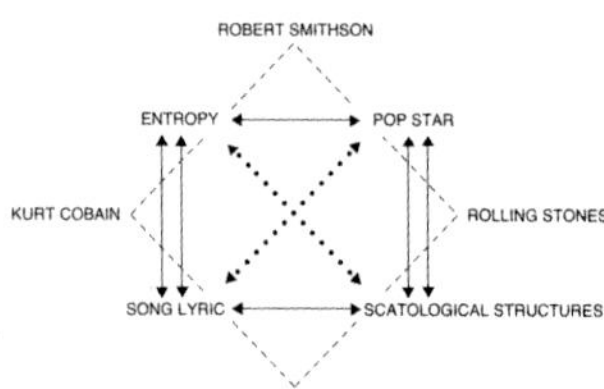

Sam Durant, Quartenary Field/Associative Diagram, 1998.

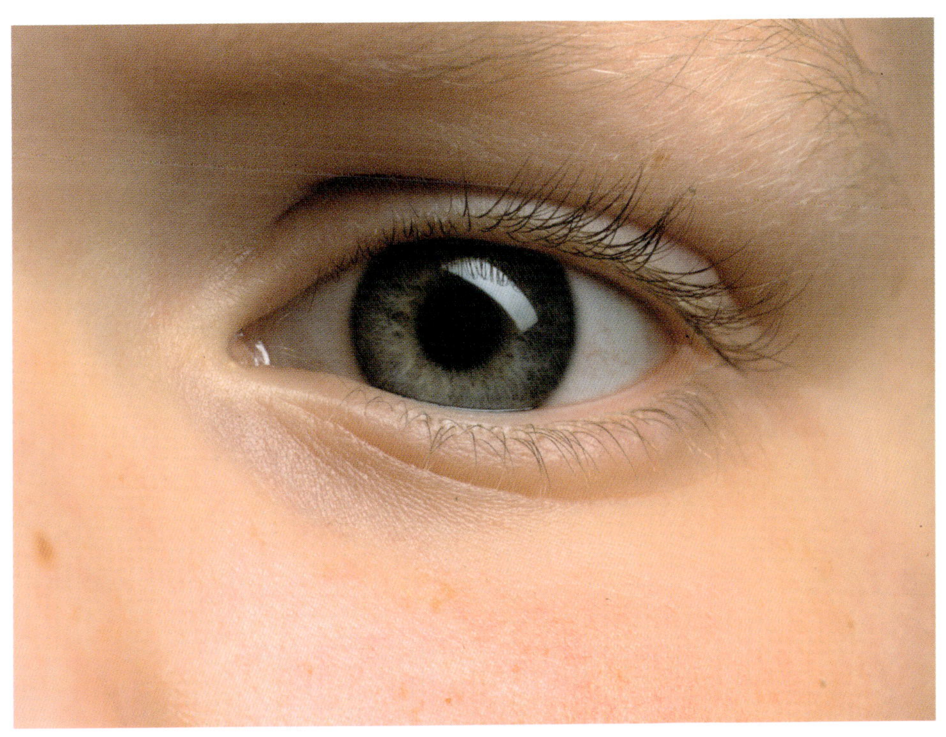

The Eye

Cibachrome   48 x 60 inches   2000

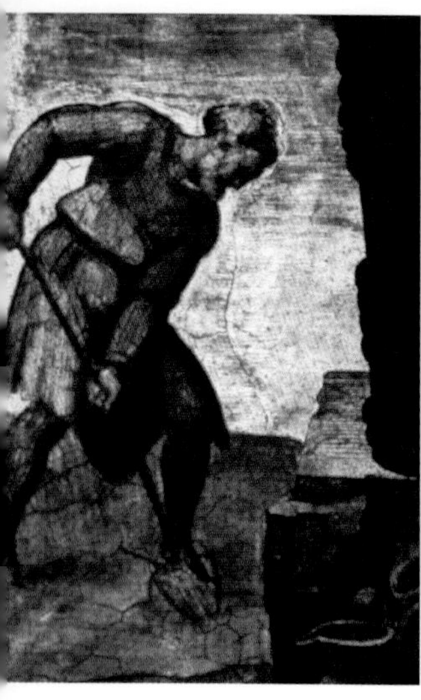

represents. Smithson is frozen in that idealized time, while Neil had to negotiate staying alive.

Who would be in your fantasy group show of all time?

Michelangelo and me.

*You could show **I Peed in My Pants**, with its combination of satisfaction, release, and shame. Your upper body is youthful confidence and control while your lower half is a mess. Incontinence or expressionism? The contradiction is what rings true.*

I love that you use the word contradiction. I think contradiction is fundamentally human.

This interview was conducted by email in fall 2002. It was expanded and edited in spring 2003.

Michelangelo, The Drunkenness of Noah (detail), 1509.

opposite: **Carving Again**
DVD   :02 loop, no sound   2000

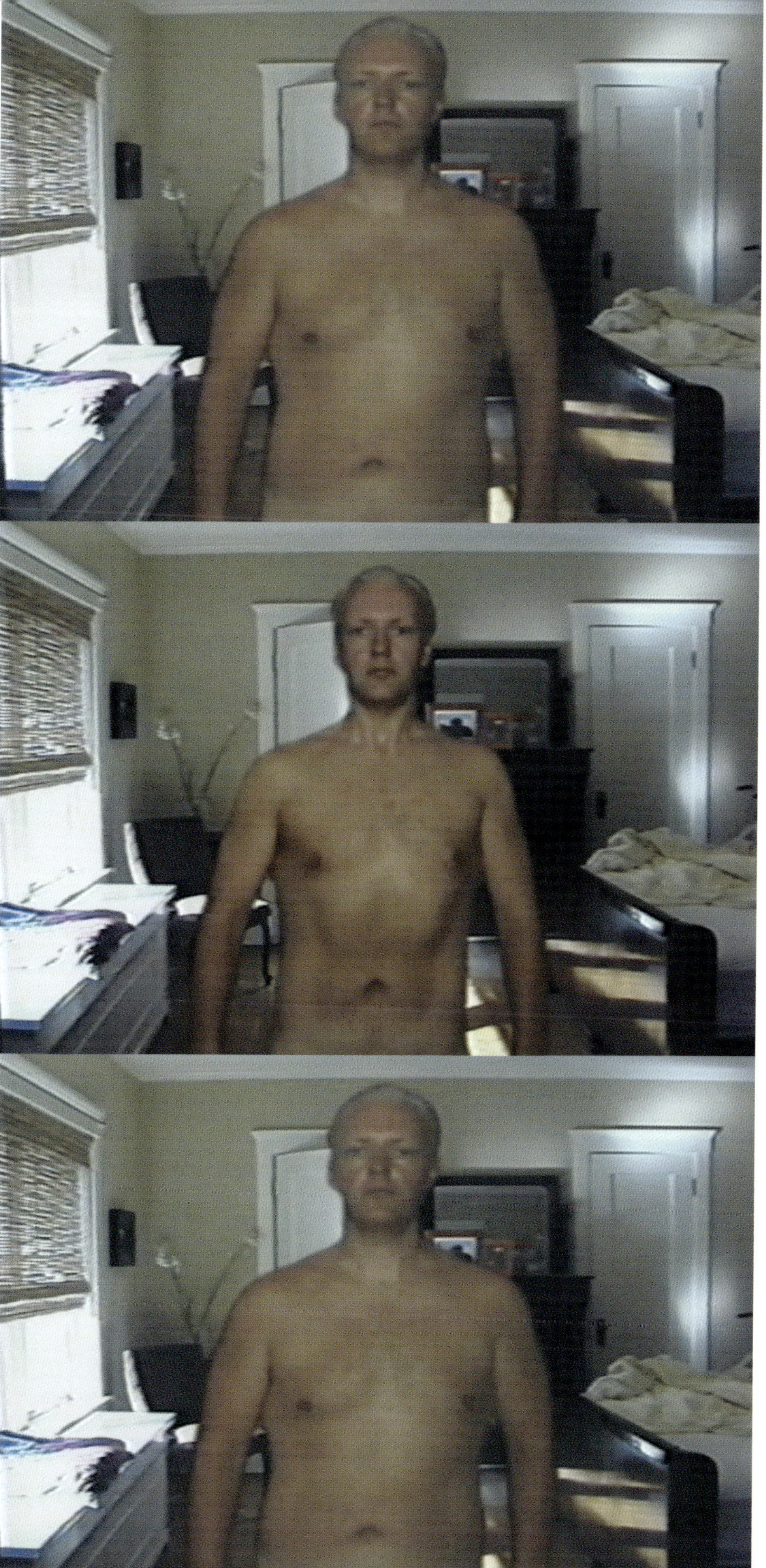

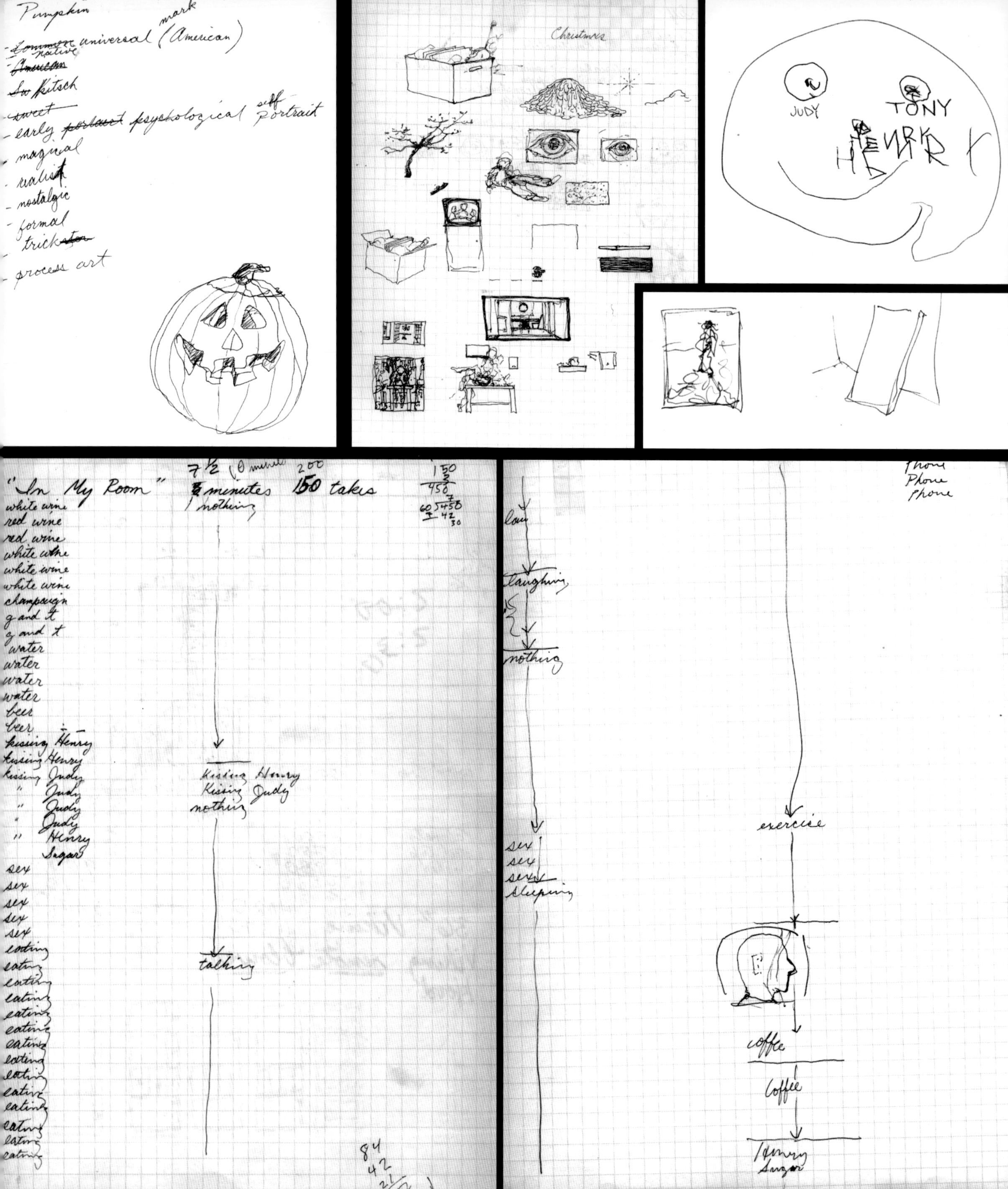

Pumpkin
- common native universal mark (American)
- American
- So Kitsch
- sweet
- early portrait psychological self portrait
- magical
- realist
- nostalgic
- formal
- trickster
- process art

Christmas

JUDY
TONY
HENRY

"In My Room"   7½ (0 minute 200
            minutes 150 takes
            nothing
white wine
red wine
red wine
white wine
white wine
white wine
champaign
g and t
g and t
water
water
water
water
beer
beer
kissing Henry
kissing Henry
kissing Judy
"   Judy
"   Judy
"   Judy
"   Henry
    Sugar
sex
sex
sex
sex
sex
eating
eating
eating
eating
eating
eating
eating
eating
eating
eating
eating
eating

Kissing Henry
Kissing Judy
nothing

talking

love

laughing

nothing

sex
sex
sex
sleeping

Phone
Phone
phone

exercise

coffee

Coffee

Henry
Sugar

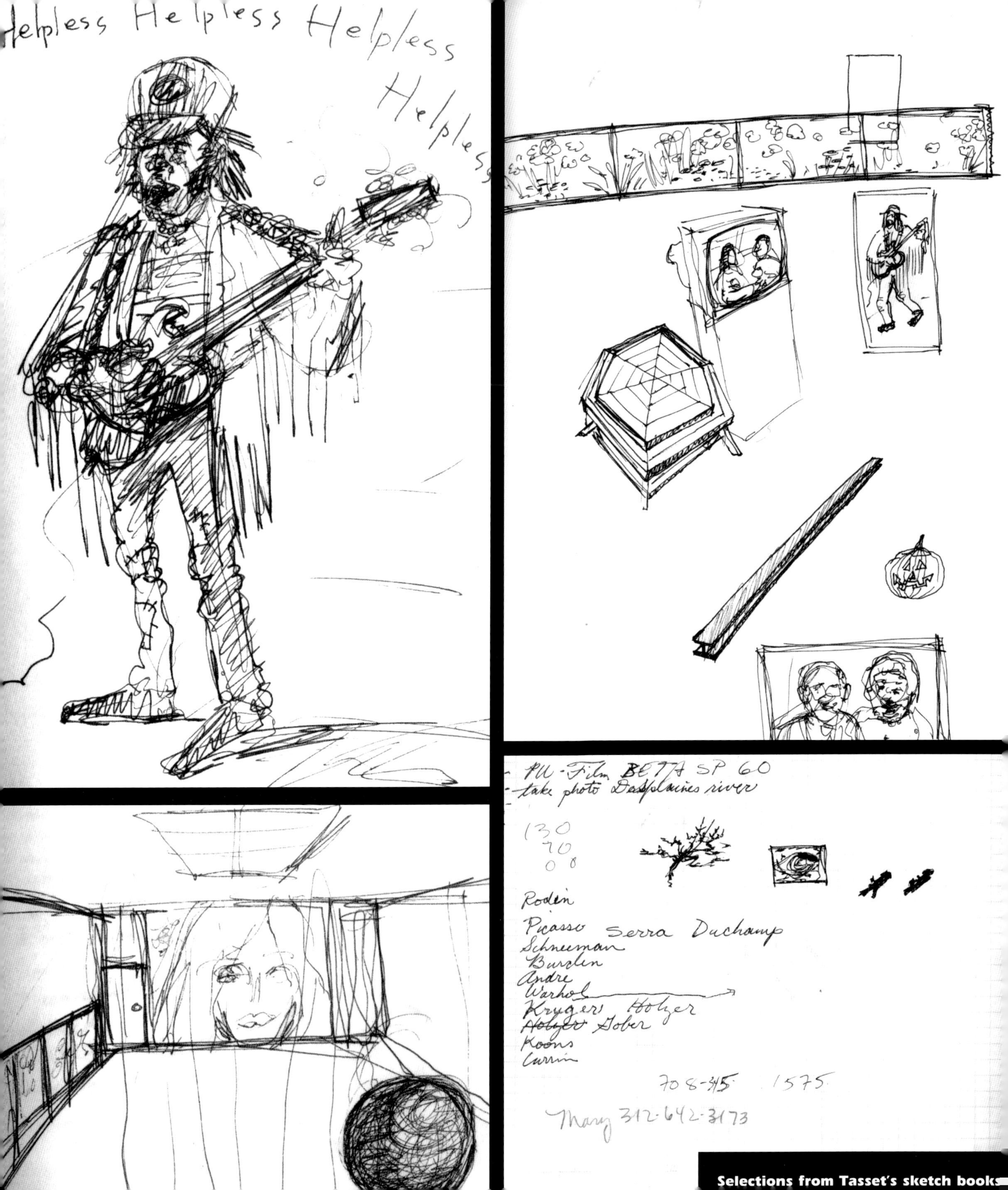

Helpless Helpless Helpless
Helpless
PU - Film BETA SP 60
take photo Desplaines river
130
70
00
Rodin
Picasso Serra Duchamp
Schneeman
Burden
Andre
Warhol
Kruger Holzer
Holzer Gober
Koons
Currin
708-345 1575
Mary 312-642-3173

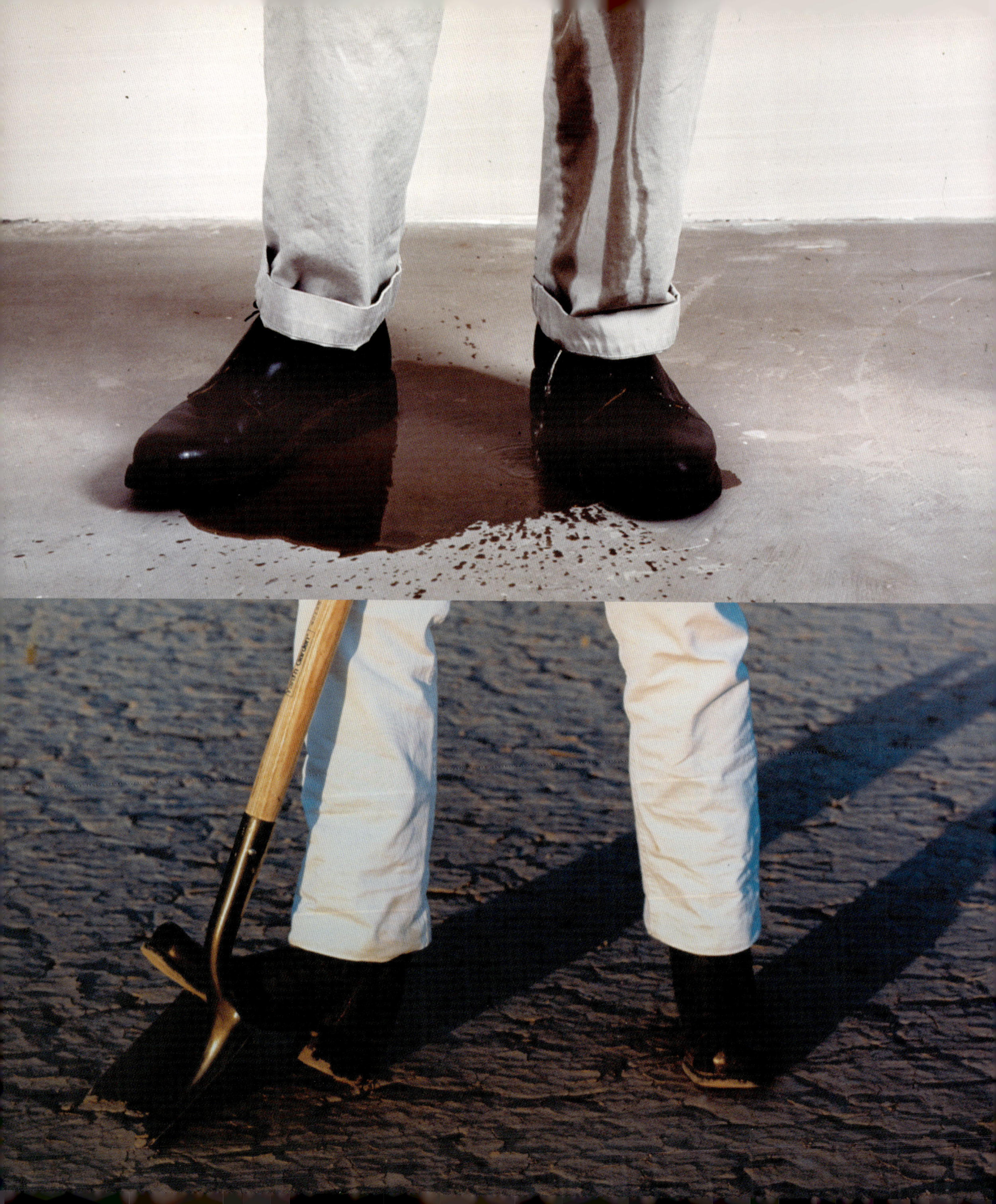

I. Anthony of the Desert

In *The Tacit Dimension*, Hungarian philosopher Michael Polanyi introduced the idea of *tacit knowledge*, stating quite simply that "we can know more than we can tell."[1] I do not think it necessarily coincidental that an artist's work should so strongly embody one of the meanings of the homophone for his last name. Tony Tasset's art is unassuming yet highly charged, spare yet laden with association.

Like Marilyn Monroe or Rock Hudson, Tony Tasset is a name that could have emerged from 50s Hollywood producer's imagination. It is a ten-letter lode of alliterative, symmetrical, near-palindromic, and etymologically enriched material just waiting to be mined. According to my American Heritage, the adjective "tony" is "marked by an elegant manner," and as a proper noun it refers to an award for outstanding theatrical achievement. "Tasset," interestingly enough, is "one of a series of jointed overlapping metal plates" used as armor for the lower trunk. Put the two words together and what you get is elegant theatrical armor—not bad for a silver-coiffed forger of hyper-precisely crafted objects, with a history of occasionally donning other artists' personas.

Continuing this line of investigation, Tasset's Christian name finds its origin in St. Anthony of Thebes, the hermetic 3rd century ascetic

Opposite above: I Peed in My Pants (detail), 1994.
Below: Robert Smithson (Las Vegas) (detail), 1995.

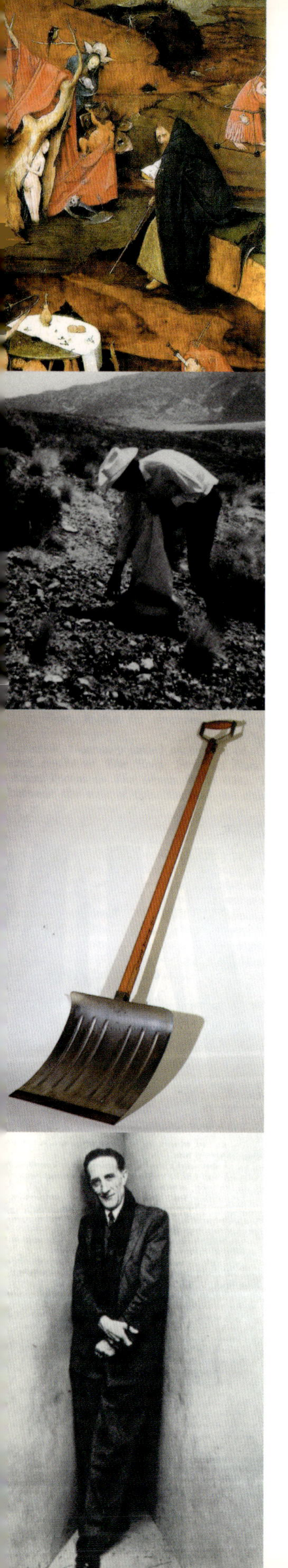

who, according to legend, lived for twenty years in an abandoned Egyptian desert fort, battling the most exquisite temptations the Devil could deal him. The desert, on the one hand, is that vast, windswept arena for self-struggle and purification, the site of Conceptual Art's most spiritually charged monuments. On the other hand, far beyond any temptation St. Anthony ever envisioned, it is the site of the monument to glitz and simulacrum that is Las Vegas. This is the very polarity the artist so tacitly ;) puts across in **Robert Smithson (Las Vegas)**, his lifesize photo-impersonation of the ascetic aesthete himself, looking more like a bookish and badly dressed 70s Elvis in Levis, clutching a spade like a mike stand.

II. Enter Marchand du Sel (Given: 1° the Waterfall)

But there is another presence haunting the Smithson picture: lurking metaphorically in the dark railway-track shadow cast by the canonized desert monk's legs is the ghost of Marcel Duchamp, the greatest shadow-caster of them all.[2] In Advance of the Broken Arm (1915), the snow shovel "chosen" by the artist who wrote the book on drag, is here reincarnated as the garden-variety shovel. From his **Comfortable Abstractions** of the mid-1980s onward, Tasset has acknowledged the pervasive influence of Duchamp on his work, borrowing freely from another artist who abhorred clutter and knew how to get volumes of effect with a minimum of effort. Tasset makes relatively little work, and many of his exhibitions have consisted of three, two, and even single works. He knows his subject so well that he has little need to shout about it. His taxidermied **Dead Blue Jay**,

Top to bottom: Heironymus Bosch, St. Anthony in Meditation (detail), c. 1500. Robert Smithson in Nevada, 1968, photo by Nancy Holt. Marcel Duchamp, In Advance of the Broken Arm, 1915. Portrait of Duchamp by Irving Penn, 1960.

for example, expresses mortality with an economic admixture of dead pan and poignancy that humbles Damien Hirst's most spectacular formaldehyde shark tank.

    In contrast to Duchamp, who according to self-propagated myth picked his readymades at random in hardware stores, Tasset would hardly claim to select his subjects with "indifference."[3] Rather, they are tenderly symbolic of the primal artistic act: the making of one's mark, whether by bronze-casting a Halloween ritual carving in **Jack-O'-Lantern**, by engaging the scatological in the life-size photograph **I Peed in My Pants** and the fecal spiral of the rusted iron **Snake**, or by recreating a snowman, that ephemeral yet ubiquitous lawn monument, in hallucinatory detail.

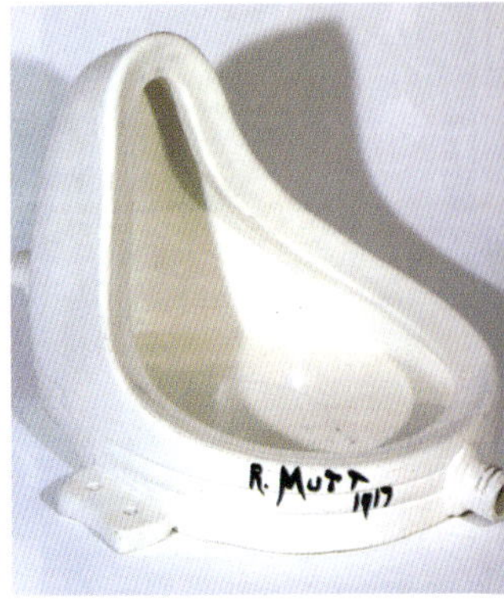

When you wet the bed first it is warm then it gets cold.
      —James Joyce, A *Portrait of the Artist as a Young Man*, 1915

The warmth of a seat (which has just been left) is infra-thin.
      —*Marcel Duchamp, Notes*, published 1980

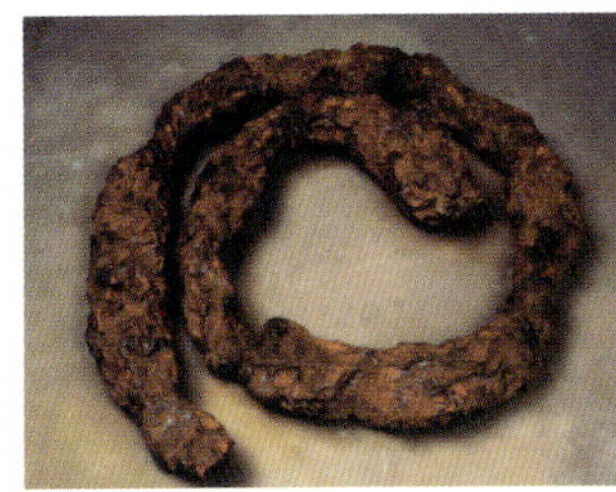

    Viewed as a pair, the fluid-based self-portrait photographs **I Peed in My Pants** and **Spew** link Tasset to Duchamp in fascinating ways. Tasset's **Spew** is a bile-laden response to the young Bruce Nauman's Self-Portrait as a Fountain, 1966-70, itself a direct reference to, and namesake of, the infamous Duchamp urinal, Fountain, of 1917. Unlike the seat retaining the warmth of the posterior just occupying it—one of several *inframinces* (commonly translated as "infrathin": "infra": under, beneath, below in a scale or series; "mince," as in

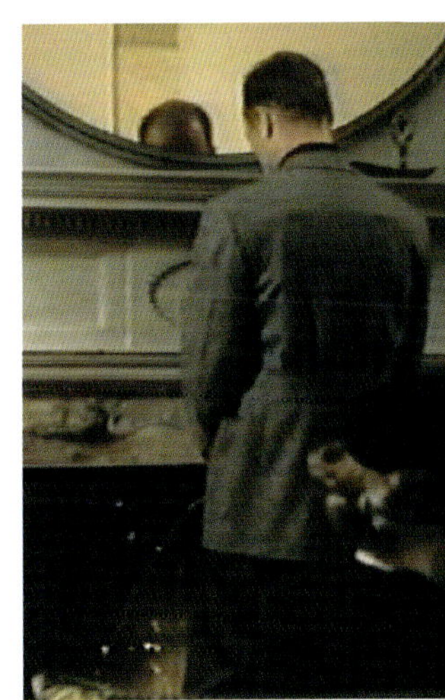

Marcel Duchamp, Fountain, 1917. Tasset, Snake, 1994. Ed Harris as Jackson Pollock in *Pollock*.

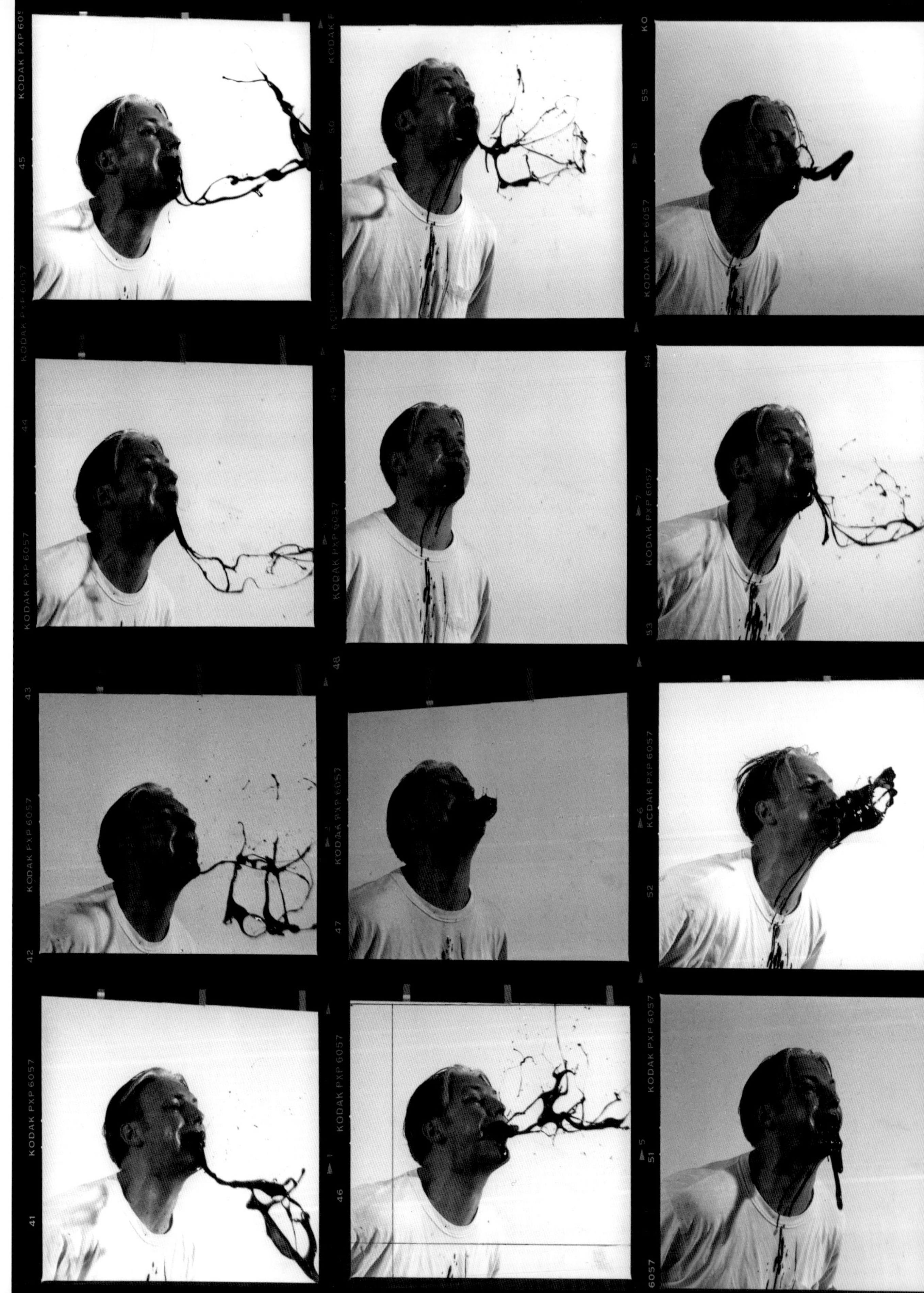

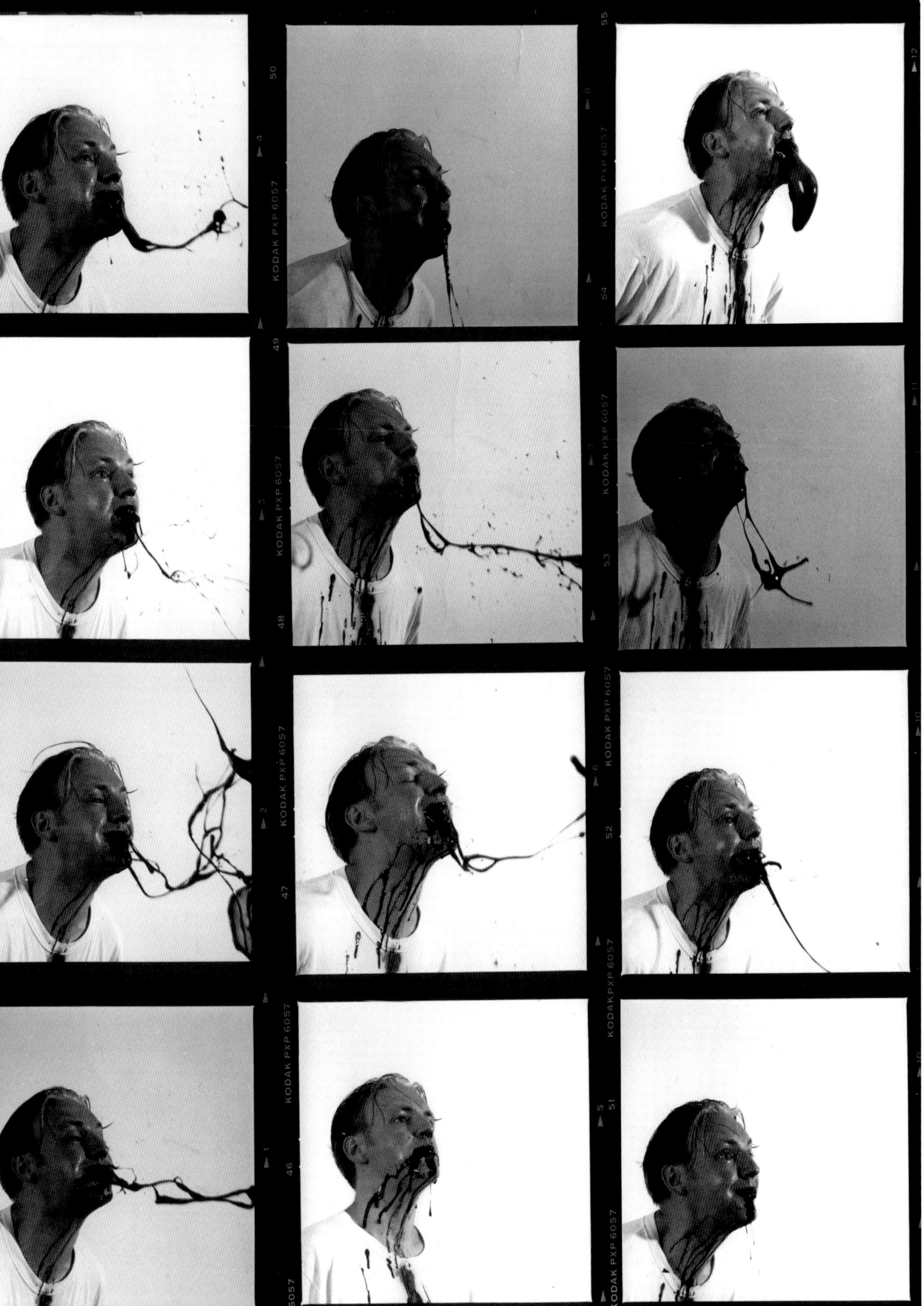

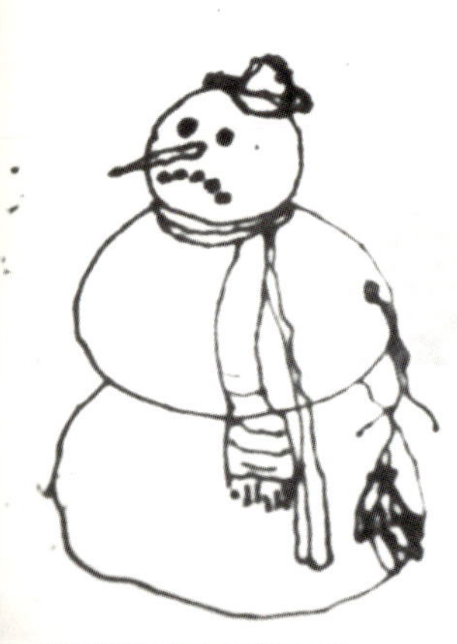

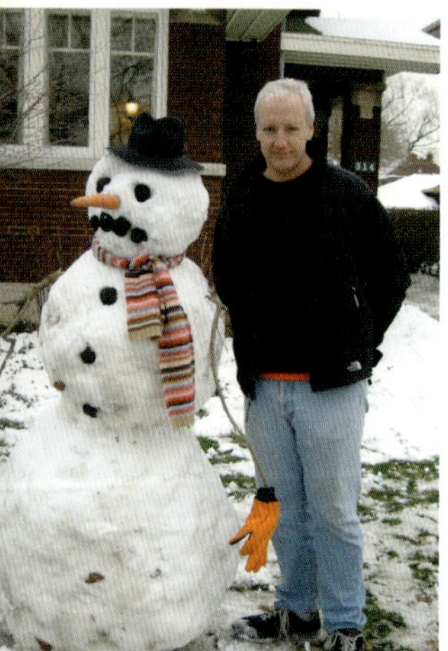

mincing words, mincing matters, speaking in a subtle or restrained [tacit?] manner, subdividing minutely) referred to in Duchamp's posthumously discovered notes—the store-bought porcelain Fountain waits in vain for the warm residue of its first deposit. Tasset goes ahead and finishes the job. In **I Peed...**, the smug, self-annointing artist displays the liquid infrathin correlate of Marcel/R. Mutt's "bathroom buddha." He presents himself as a human readymade, standing in a puddle of urine, retaining in his soaked trousers the dissipating heat of his own "body fountain."

III. A Winter's Tale

The possible implying the becoming—the passage from one to the other takes place in the infrathin.

The difference (dimensional) between 2 mass produced objects [from the same mold] is an infra thin when the maximum (?) precision is obtained.
—Marcel Duchamp, Notes

Just as **I Peed...** realizes the bodily reference in Fountain, Tasset's **Snowman** responds to the sculptural implications of In Advance of the Broken Arm's instructional title. Following infrathin logic, using Duchamp's snow shovel would invariably result in many "cast" snow objects, each retaining to a greater or lesser degree the imprint of the shovel/mold.[4]

When I drove up to Oak Park with Bill Conger last December, I was expecting to return with an armful of slides, photos and notes from Tasset's private stash. But Tony had other plans: while the three of us stood in his studio looking at his tiny felt-tip drawing of a pathetic frowning snowman, he

Snowman sketch. Tasset with snowman, Oak Park, December 2002.

proposed that we build a snowman together on his front lawn to use as a prototype for a new sculpture. Although it was freezing out, we felt obliged to indulge him, wondering if it was a foil to secretly videotape Bill and me traipsing around in the snow and use *that* for a new art piece.

It was too cold for any sizable snowball to hold together, so I got the bright idea of hooking up his garden hose to wet the snow, which provided the necessary adhesion. (I was thinking I should have kept my mouth shut, soon realizing that I had volunteered my services as a superfluous lawn irrigator *and* human snow shovel—recalling simultaneously Duchamp's Fountain and In Advance of a Broken Arm. Digging away at an "earthwork"—a wet version of the Smithson desert photo—we rolled three icy boulders all over the lawn, picking up grass, leaves, mud, and yellow snow along the way. Within an hour we had created the actual-sized model for a sculpture he would finish just in time for the opening of his January show in Normal. It had charcoal eyes, mouth and buttons, the usual carrot nose, and drooping tree-branch arms outfitted with mismatched gloves. Think of it: two curators and an artist, making a child's outdoor sculpture.[5]

A snowman is a winter scarecrow, a talismanic guardian figure for suburban lawns, ubiquitously reproduced on Christmas cards, giftwrap, and even postage stamps. Seeing an incredibly detailed copy of something so ephemeral, yet so *sculptural*—about the simplest sculpture you could possibly make, one that anyone living in a climate with snow has made—caused me to think about what distinguishes Iasset's **Snowman** from the thousands of similar

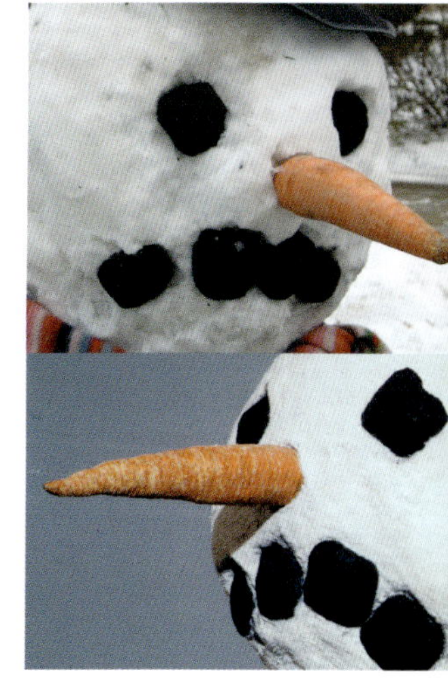

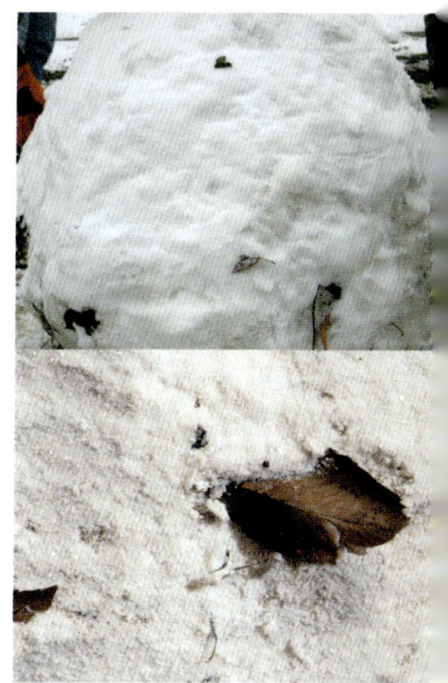

Detail of Oak Park snowman. Detail of Snowman, 2003. Detail of Oak park snowman. Detail of Snowman.

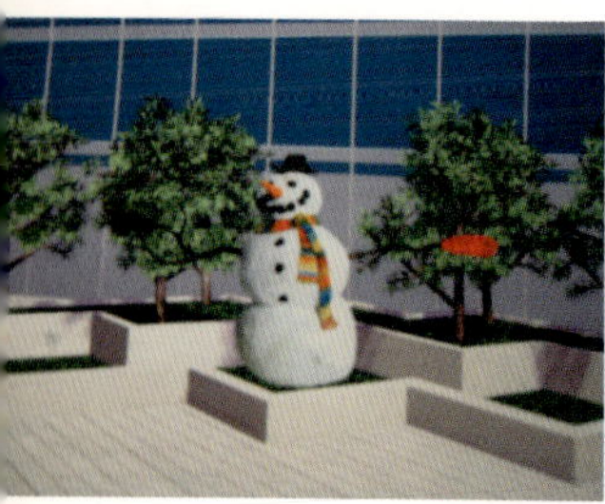

Christmas display figures in upper-tier stores across America.

First of all, like **Cherry Tree** and **Jack-O'-Lantern**, it is ingeniously crafted—consisting of plaster-coated foam body, wax arms, Sculpey facial features, and painted metal leaves and grass—and it is shockingly real. Secondly, it is a portrait of an icon, like Neil Young, only way older. (Unfortunately, no archeological record exists for what could well be one of the first generic figural sculptures ever fashioned.) And finally, it is a portrait of not just *any* snowman, but the one we made together that December day—a poor-postured one whose downcast arms echo not only the curve of its frowning mouth, but the tenor of our bleak, pre-war winter 2002 zeitgeist as well. For me, a snowman will never again be just a snowman. That's the magical transformation that happens whenever an artist succeeds in re-envisioning the ordinary.

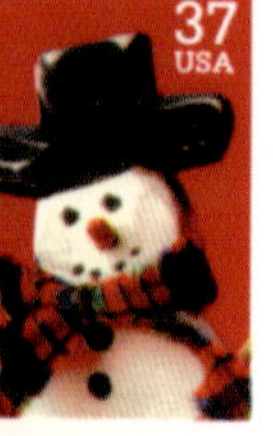
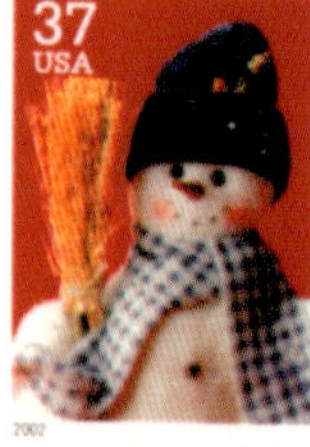
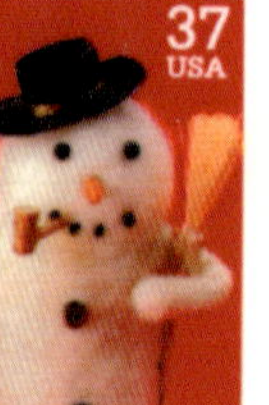
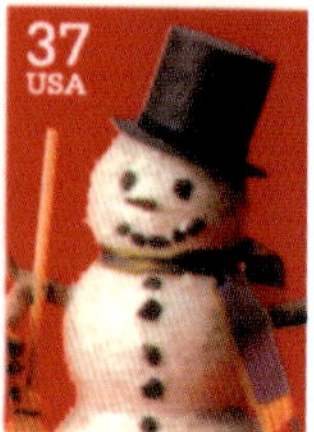

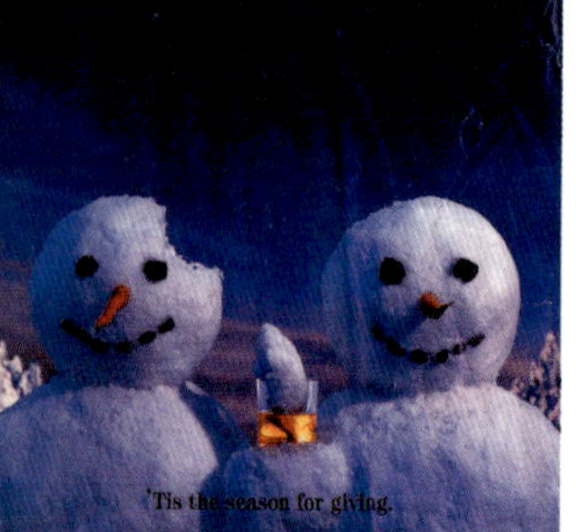

Tasset, proposal for LaSalle Bank. U. S. Postage stamps. Crown Royal advertisement.

Endnotes

1. Michael Polanyi, *The Tacit Dimension*, Garden City, NY: Anchor Books, 1967.

2. Like many in his circle, Duchamp was fascinated by theories concerning the fourth dimension. In Note 3, p. 36 in his *Notes and Projects for the Large Glass*, Abrams, 1969, the artist states that "the shadow cast by a 4-dimensional figure on our space is a 3-dimensional shadow." Another reference to shadow-casting can be found in *Marcel Duchamp, Notes*, Georges Pompidou Center, 1980: "'Shadow-caster' a company of shadow casters represented by all the sources of light (sun, moon, stars, candles, fire—)." Traced shadows cast by three of his readymades appear in his largest painting on canvas, Tu m', 1918.

3. In *Dialogues with Marcel Duchamp* by Pierre Cabanne, Da Capo edition, 1987, p. 48, Duchamp states "...You have to approach something with an indifference, as if you had no aesthetic emotion. The choice of readymades is always based on visual indifference and, at the same time, on the total absence of good or bad taste."

4. As fate would have it, "arm" can mean armor, or tasset.

5. Of course, this left no time to look through Tasset's archive of photos, press, catalogues, and notebooks. I did, however, get to visit Judy Ledgerwood's studio (Tasset occupies the ground floor, Judy the second) to view three big paintings uncharacteristically done in just black and white. They were severe, minimal, very strong. A temporary purging of color, as in the careers of DeKooning and Pollock.

It struck me as more than a little curious that another big Minimalist black-and-white artwork she hadn't yet seen was now standing in her front yard. Their concerns as artists have always been quite divergent—she the Modernist, he the PoMo conceptualist—but can you live with another artist for twenty years without exerting some sort of gravitational force on each other's art?

Maybe it was the effect of the snow hitting my windshield head-on, the light-deprivation of the endless Illinois winter, or just a curator's endless quest for affinities, but over the next few trips to Oak Park I began to fixate on a pervasive black-and-white theme going on in the Tasset-Ledgerwood household. Examples: one of Tony's early framed hide pieces, resembling both a detail of his dalmation Sugar and the large spot patterns Judy happened to be painting on ceramic plates and cups. The retro Kitty kitchen clock , the aforementioned snowman and paintings, and the two dressed in black and white on the same day.

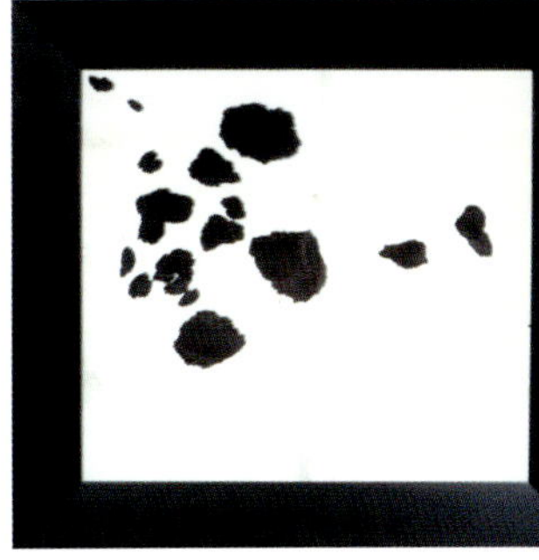

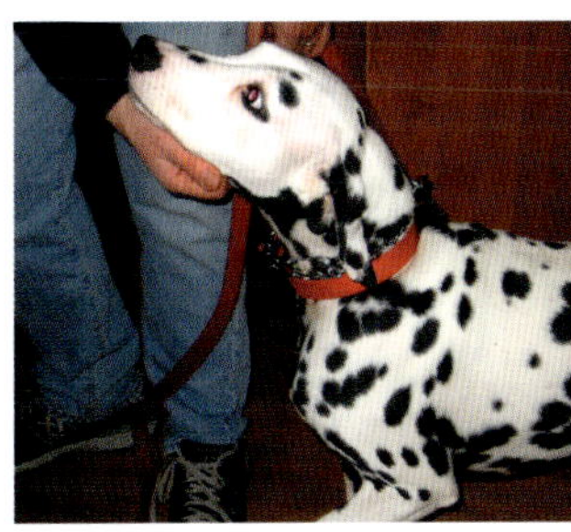

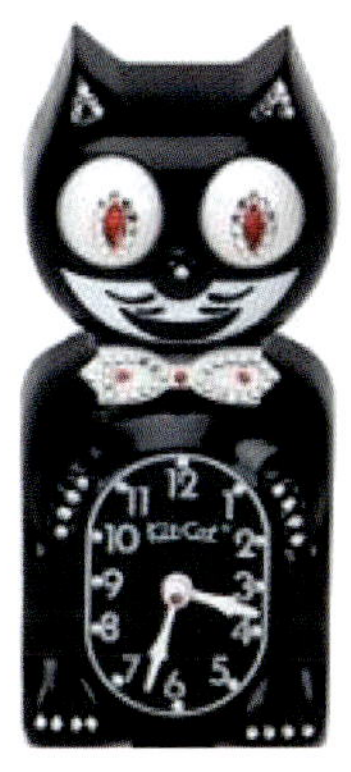

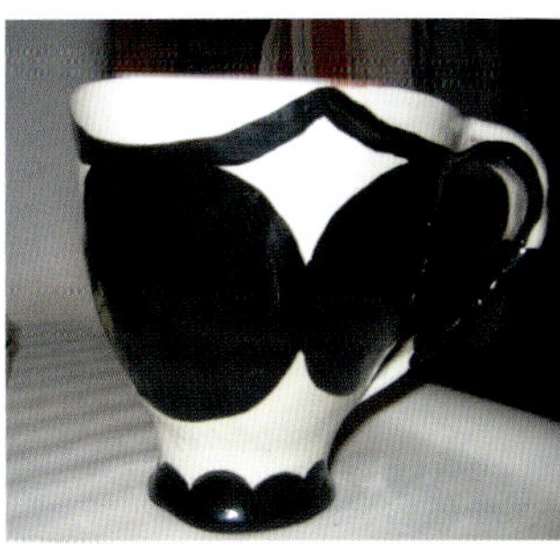

Tasset, Domestic Abstraction, 1987. Sugar. Tasset's kitchen clock. Ceramic cup by Nancy Gardner, painted by Judy Ledgerwood.

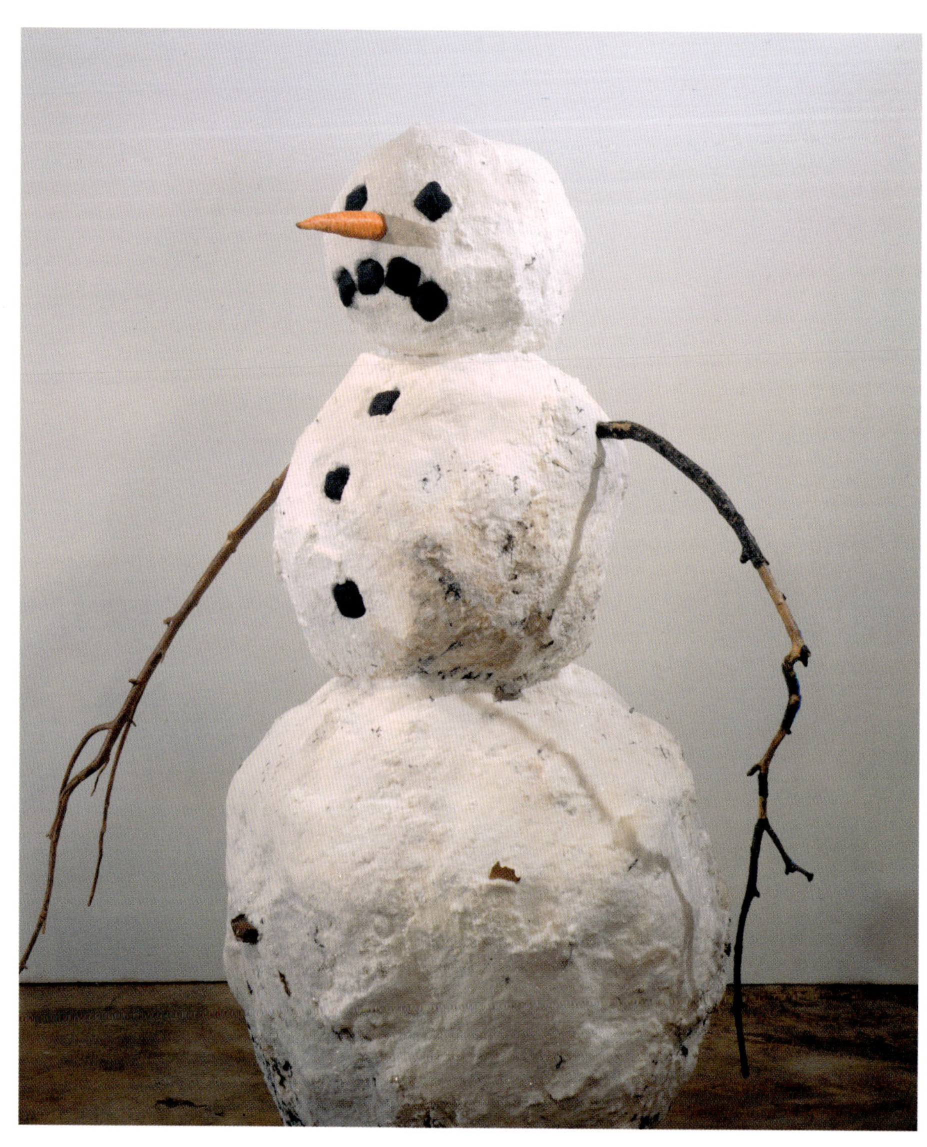

Snowman

Polystyrene, fiberglass mesh, paper-mache, plaster, Sculpey, wax, steel, brass, acrylic
beads, fake snow, acrylic and oil paint   71 x 55 x 40 inches   2003

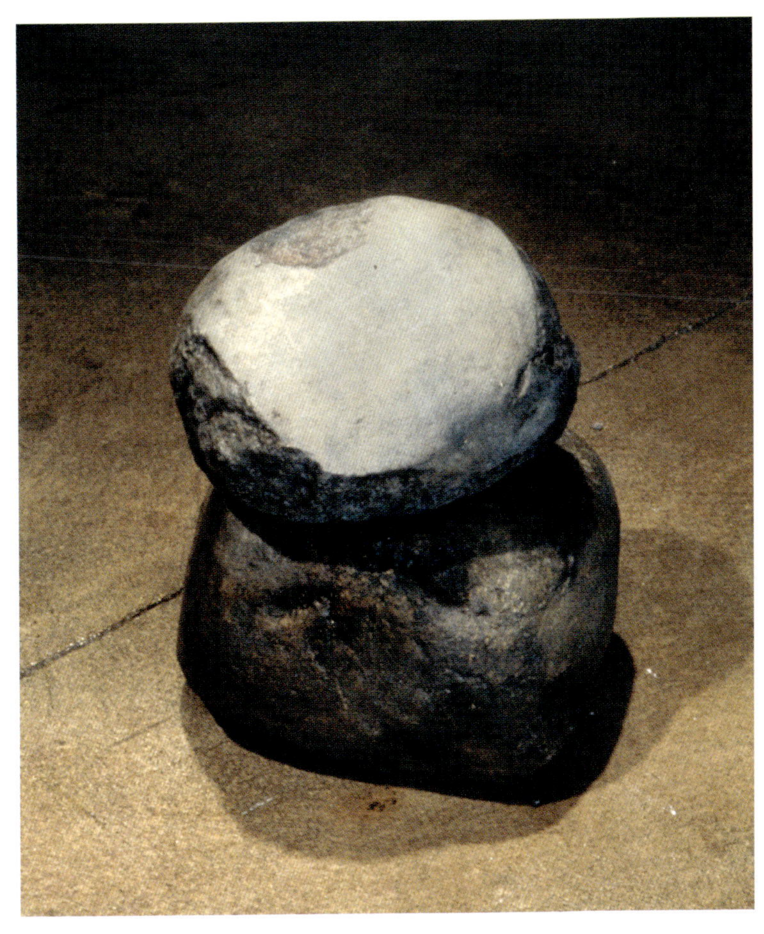

Marker

Oil paint on Ultracal   15 x 13 x 12 inches   2000

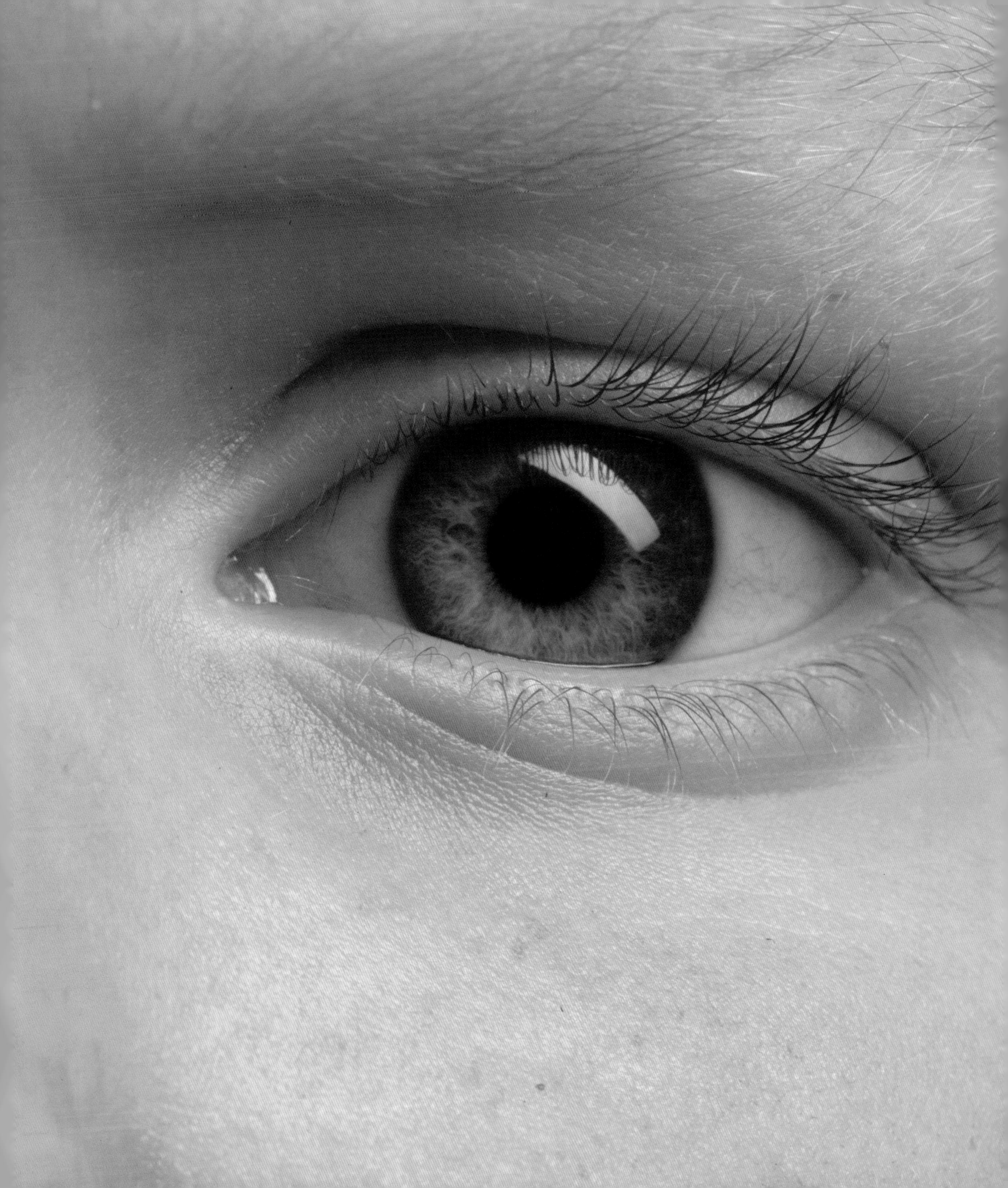

Michelle Grabner

Tony Tasset's **The Eye**, a tightly cropped and vastly enlarged photograph of a child's single blue-gray eye, summons wonderment, purity and goodness. It is iconic, obviously a surrogate, as these Platonic ideals are not of the physical world. But there is something else at play here, something less benign and less perfect, and maybe even a little sad. It is the artist himself, and the subject of Tasset's work since 1993.

Tasset navigates the world cognitively, unable to remove the critical filters that shadow his existence. The pleasures that life affords him as an artist, father, husband and professor are churned through a complex psychological rubric of self-examination, social analysis and cultural critique. He perpetually struggles to see the world as absolute, free from irony and doubt, the way a child sees branches on a tree or pumpkins in the fall. But he cannot.

Looking back on Tasset's oeuvre, **Spew**, a photograph from 1993, marks a critical turn in his focus. This image, depicting a projectile-vomiting Tasset, marks the end of a body of work that investigated the inherent cultural values of art itself: authorship, display, craft and originality. But **Spew** also marks a turn inward. In this photograph we begin to see Tasset as a corporeal being, an organic body with guttural urges. It is a turning away from art as subject matter.

After **Spew** Tasset pees his pants, sculpts turd-like objects, and role-plays in an attempt to locate what is inherently human, immediate

Opposite: The Eye (detail), 2000.

and self-gratifying in life. After seven years of working through theory-driven simulationist strategies, Tasset explores the id and the critical stages in human development associated with instinctual impulses, unregulated by the influences of reason. Although his subject has changed, Tasset's interest in the simulacrum as a viable visual language, ripe with Baudrillardian critique, remains evident.

And then it happens. With a straightforward photographic portrait of his parents, smiling and dressed in their Sunday best, Tasset ushers in a personal dimension that forever changes the philosophical location of his work. Past hierarchies are realigned and his relationship to art and success becomes confused. Call it a mid-life crisis, call it what you like, but this is when it gets good. With this photograph, Tasset sets out on a path of coming to know the world from local coordinates: the suburb, the family, the upper middle class, the educated liberal.

The psychological dimension in Tasset's work is rich, embracing issues of nature and nurture, biological determinism, gender and moral relativism. Objects and images from his everyday life are regularly scrutinized for their unknowing role in the makeup of his psycho-social identity. Nothing is too mundane or too pop to escape his incrimination. Ordinary encounters and familiar experiences consistently get snagged in his critical sieve. A flowering tree, a dead bird, his wife, his son, breakfast—all of these things pose critical challenges and ethical obstacles for Tasset.

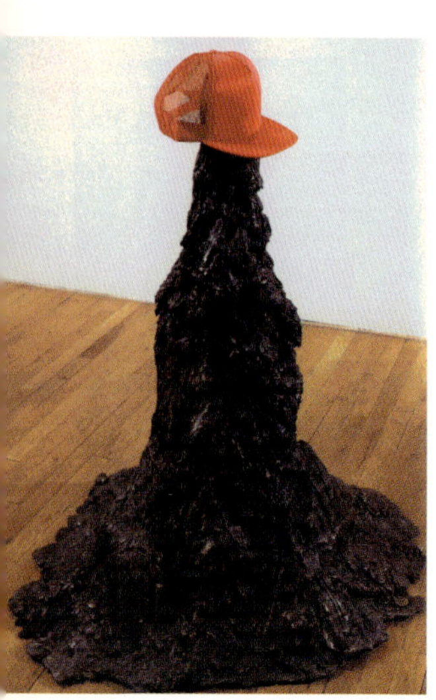

Tasset, Abstraction with Hat, 1994.

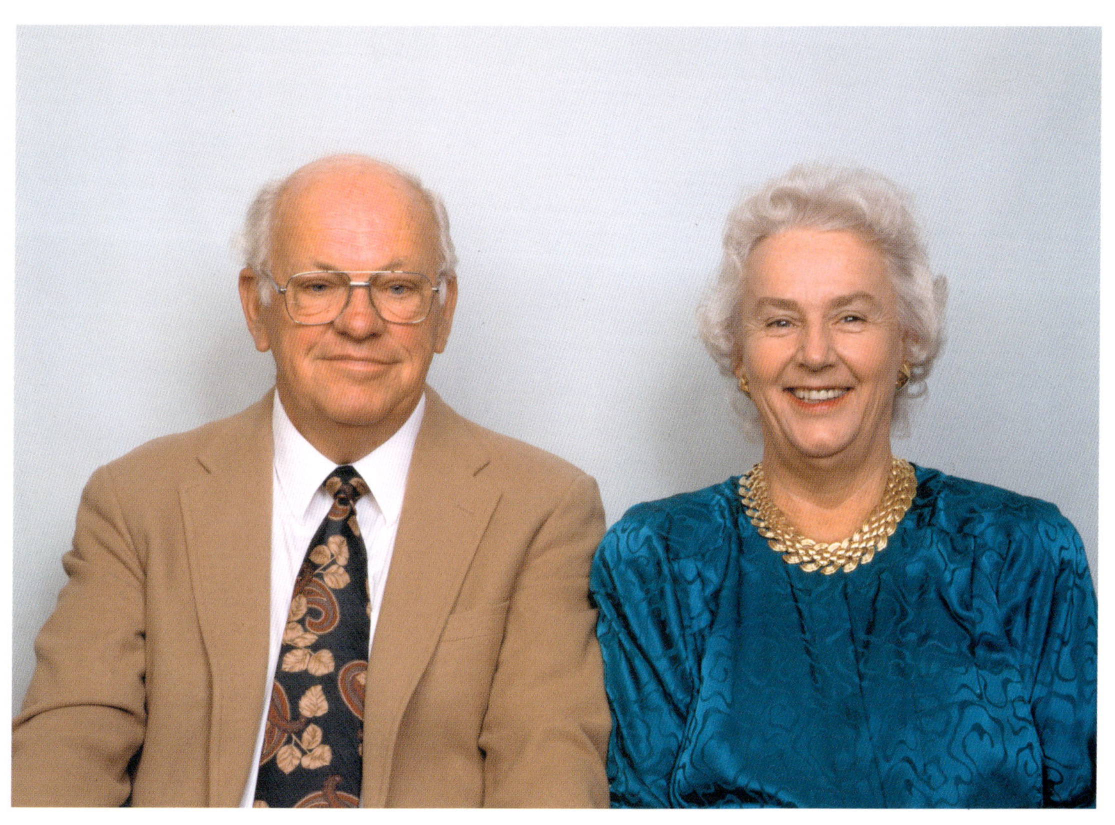

My Parents

Cibachrome   52 x 72 inches   1994

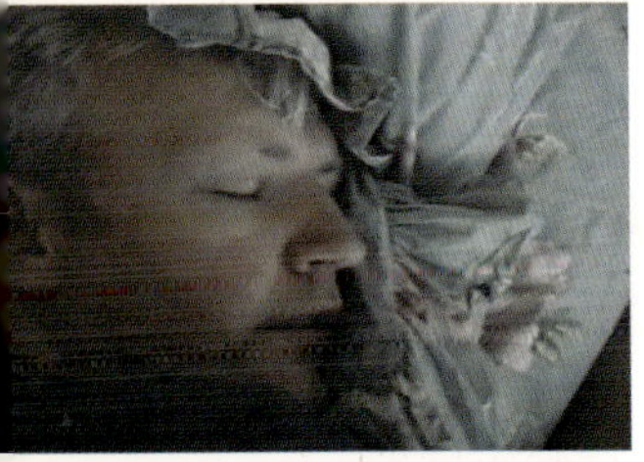

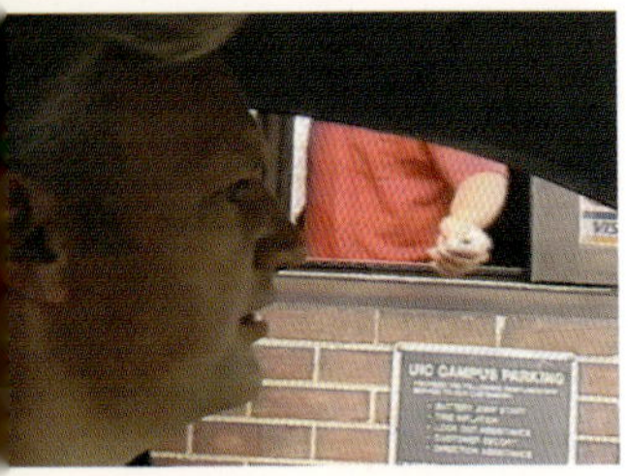

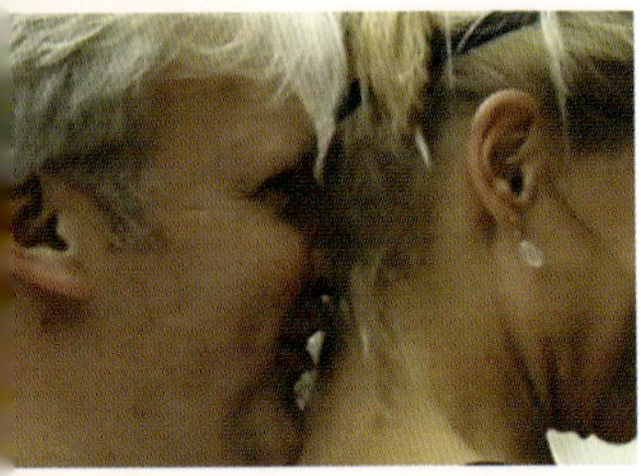

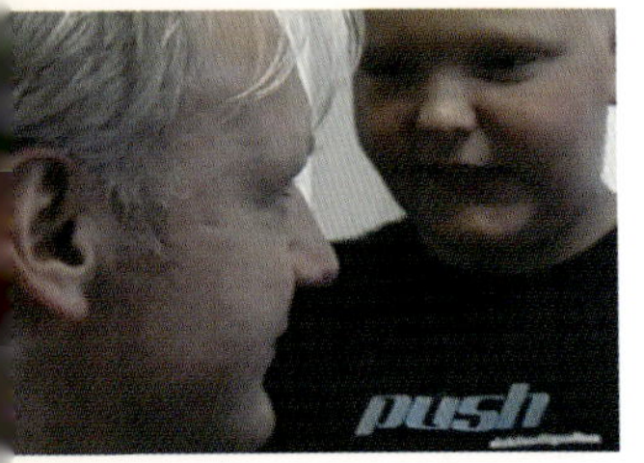

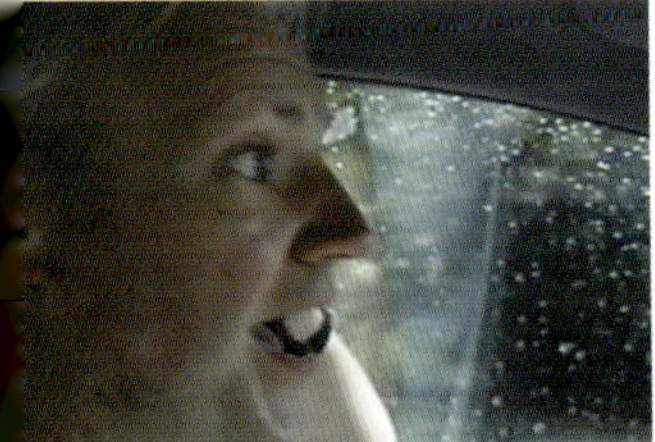

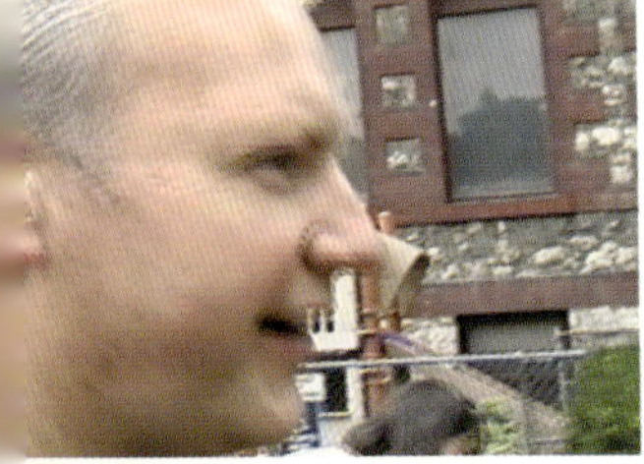

In My Room, a video that indexes his everyday life, objectively maps the subject, Tasset, as he eats, shits, goes to the hardware store or the post office, advises students, fills his car with gasoline, and smells a peony in his garden. Compositionally, one half of each image comprising this video is occupied by the artist's profile. The other half, the right side, reveals the other stuff. Yet this split is not harmonious, it is empirical. We witness Tasset slipping between personal activities and social ones but the effect is not voyeuristic. **In My Room** could just as well be titled "In My Head"—what we don't see, the cognitive processing of these activities, is the true measure of Tasset's being. Meaningfulness, intelligibility and coherence are flattened when every activity in his day is recorded. It is only in Tasset's head that this string of discontinuous stimuli is filtered, assembled, grouped and categorized into something whole.

Does our brain perceive objects, or does it conceive them? This is a question that was posed in reference to Magritte's work by French author Marcel Jean in 1959, and it is a question fundamental to Tasset's work today. His painted bronze jack-o'-lantern, taxidermied blue jay, and painted-wax cherry tree evoke an illusion of realism that is not only surreal in nature but verges on "hysterical realism," a term recently employed by literary critic James Wood, characterizing a genre of contemporary literary works by authors such as David Foster Wallace. In Wood's view, Wallace is "a kind of Frankfort School entertainer—a cultural theorist, fighting culture with dialectical devilry." Tasset's objects are visually equivalent to this style of writing. They are epic yet anxiety ridden, vital and over-

Video stills from In My Room, 2000.

worked, intellectual and superficial.

Take for example **Snowman**, a life-size sparkling figure with a carrot nose and a sad, downturned charcoal mouth. From the painted wax arms to the brass leaves and debris folded into the layers of "snow," the illusionism of this figure is truly excessive, even manic, in an attempt to simulate the real. As a ubiquitous pop character, the snowman represents an ideal, rational figure whose spherical geometry is absolute and perfect. Yet the pathos this figure solicits comes from its temporary condition: it is a man of snow after all. Tasset's snowman is impervious to temperature, yet his immortal character is still visibly unhappy. Like the blue jay, jack-o'-lantern and cherry tree, **Snowman**, exemplifies how Tasset teases out complexities, paradoxes and metaphors that emotionally confuse a viewer's relationship to the normal and the trite.

Beauty has also taken on a compelling role in Tasset's cognitive reach for pleasure and acts of pure perception. He understands beauty as a concept, but it is difficult for him to see . So he compensates by giving us images of his wife, an abstract painter whose relationship to beauty is firsthand. She cultivates it in her studio and garden and she lives within it gracefully without interrogating its ontology. He also gives us an image of his son's eye (**The Eye**), an eye that perceives the world heteronomously. **Big Eye**, a perversely gigantic sculpture of a disembodied all-seeing eye—this time his own—also presents viewers with an ocular instrument. Unlike Luis Bunuel and Salvador Dali's gesture to strike out at visual perception by slicing an eye in the 1929 film *Un Chien Andalou*, Tasset gives

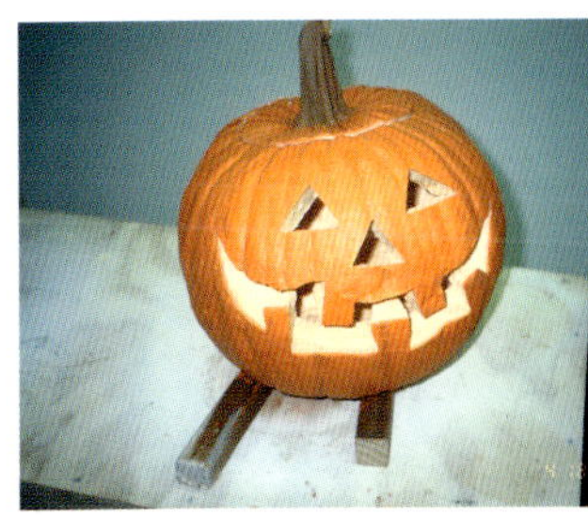

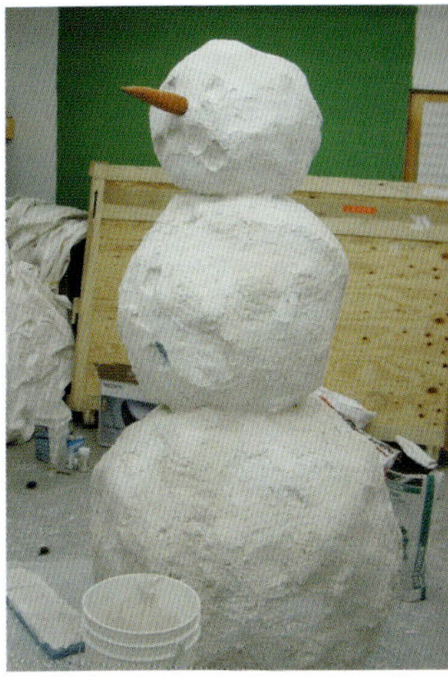

Tasset, Jack-O'-Lantern in production, 1997. Snowman in production, 2002.

us a surrogate colossal lens in a futile attempt to magnify the beauty, pleasure and goodness that comprises his life.

In its entirety, Tasset's work weaves a narrative about a conceptual artist who is perceptually handicapped. In conflict with the habitual modes of understanding the world, he does not let the mere facts of life be. He can cunningly identify pleasure and beauty but he seems only able to engage in them through critique and cultural context. Tasset crafts exquisite objects and creates profound images, continuing the post-conceptual tradition of cognitive inquiry. But everything in his world is fair game. He leaves nothing for himself.

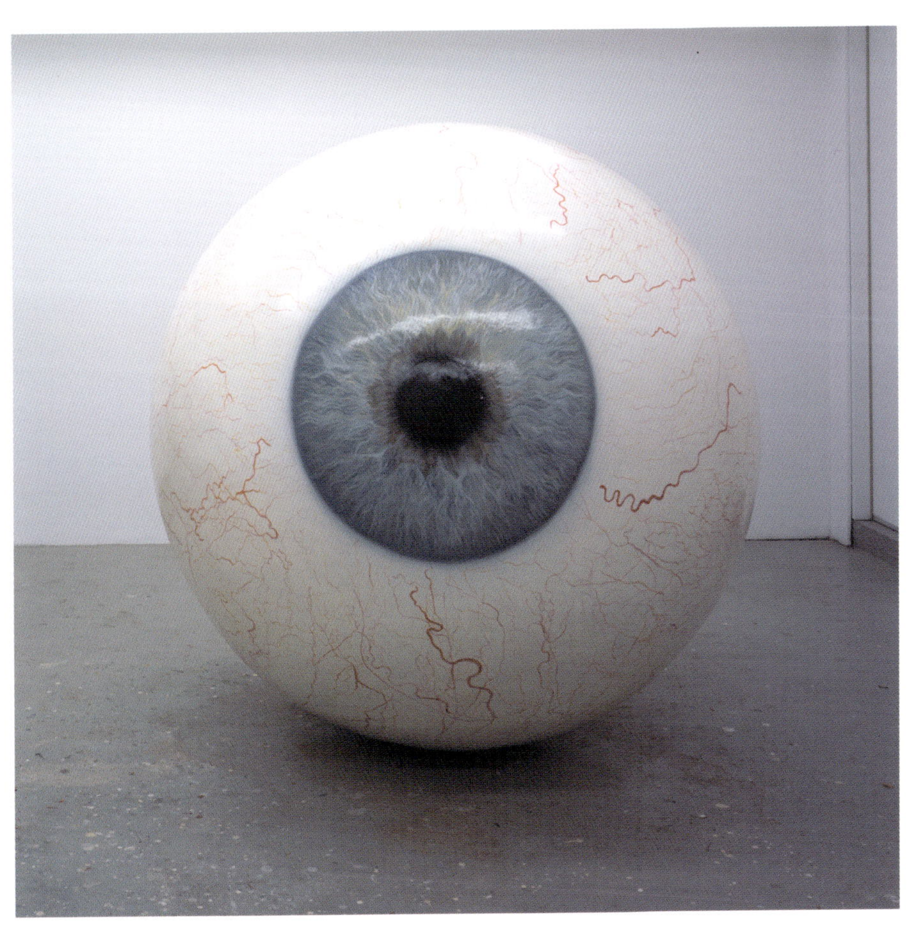

Big Eye

Polystyrene, latex cement, and acrylic paint   60-inch spheroid   2001

Frederick R. Weisman Art Foundation

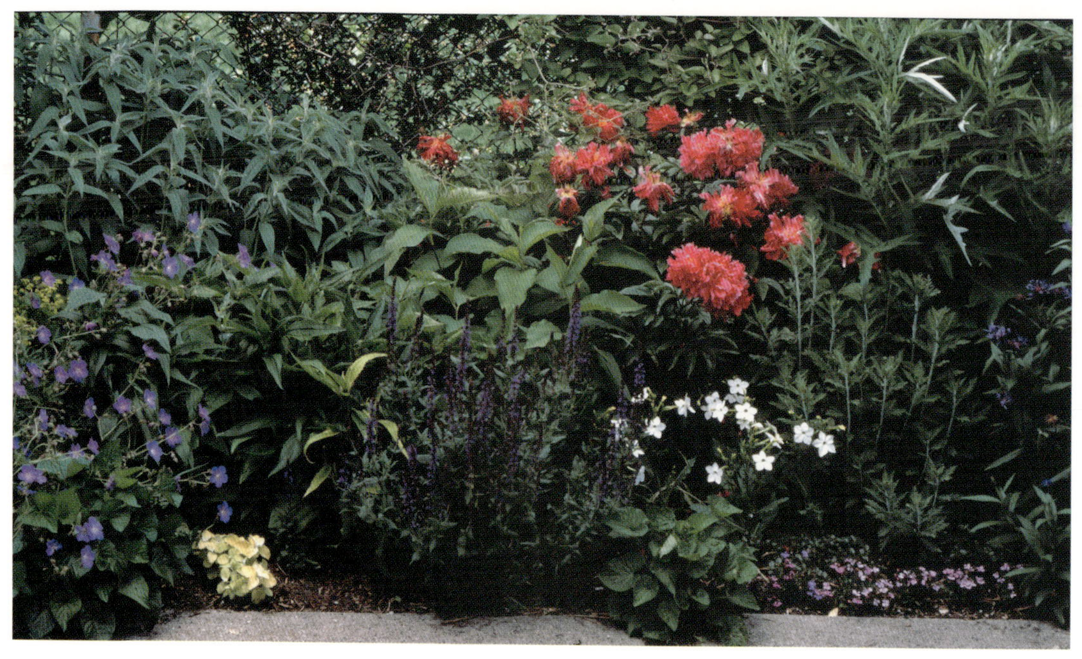

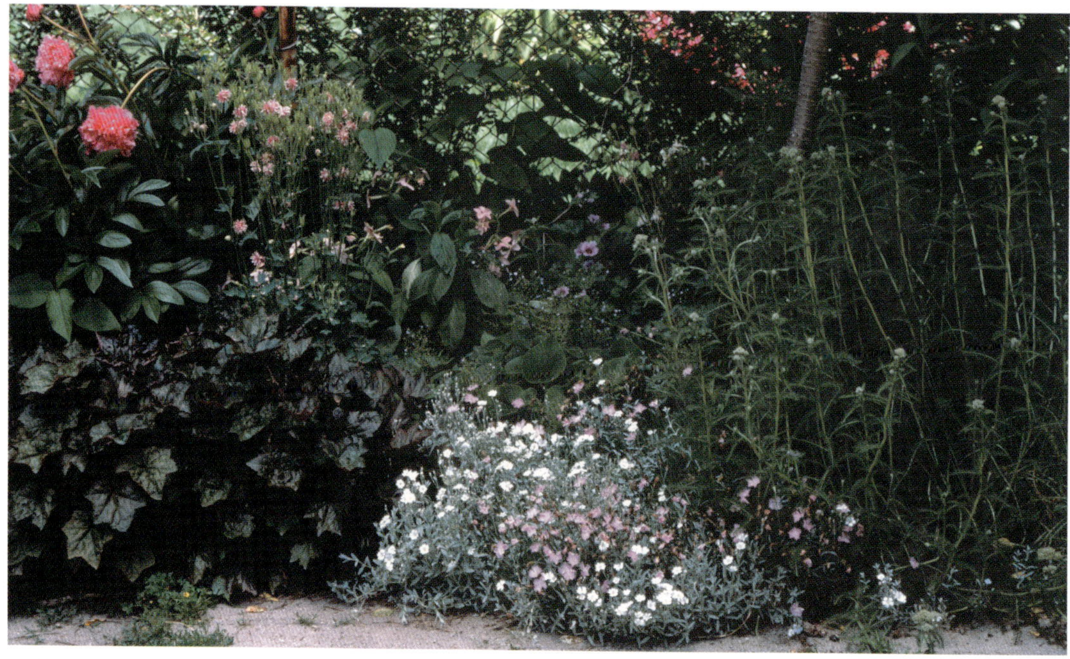

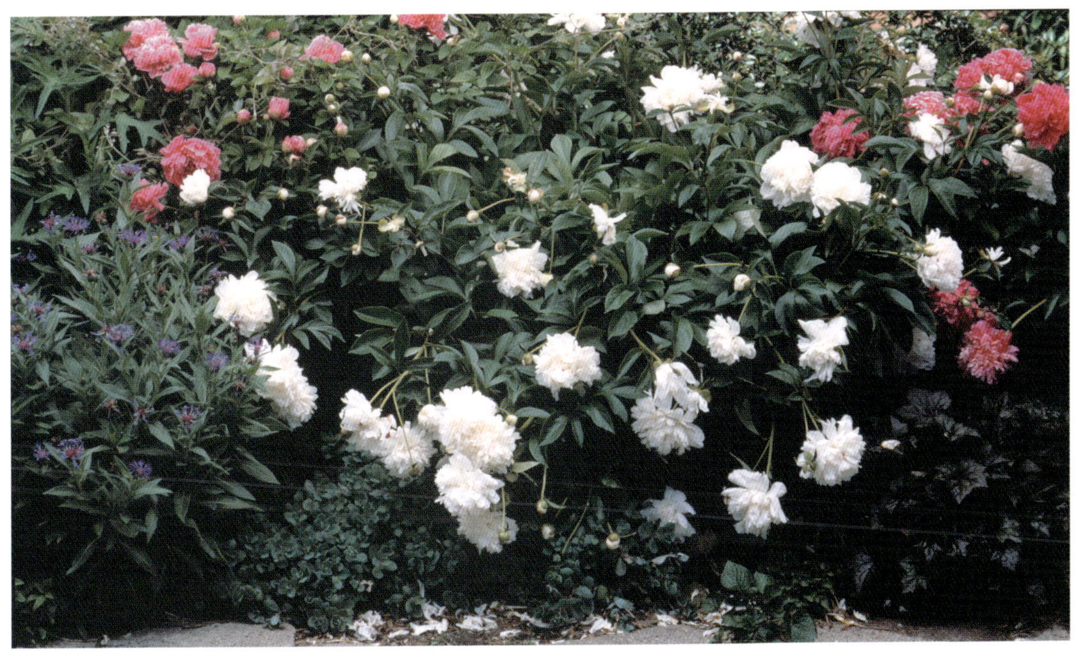

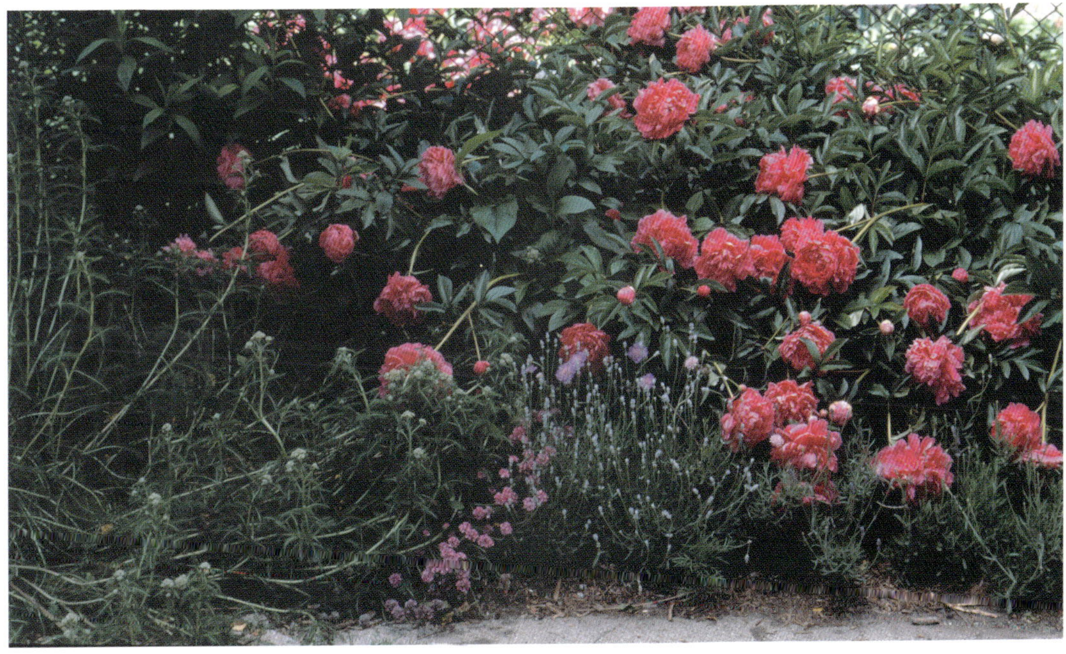

My Garden

Cibachrome   4 panels, 48 x 84 inches each, 48 x 336 inches installed   1993

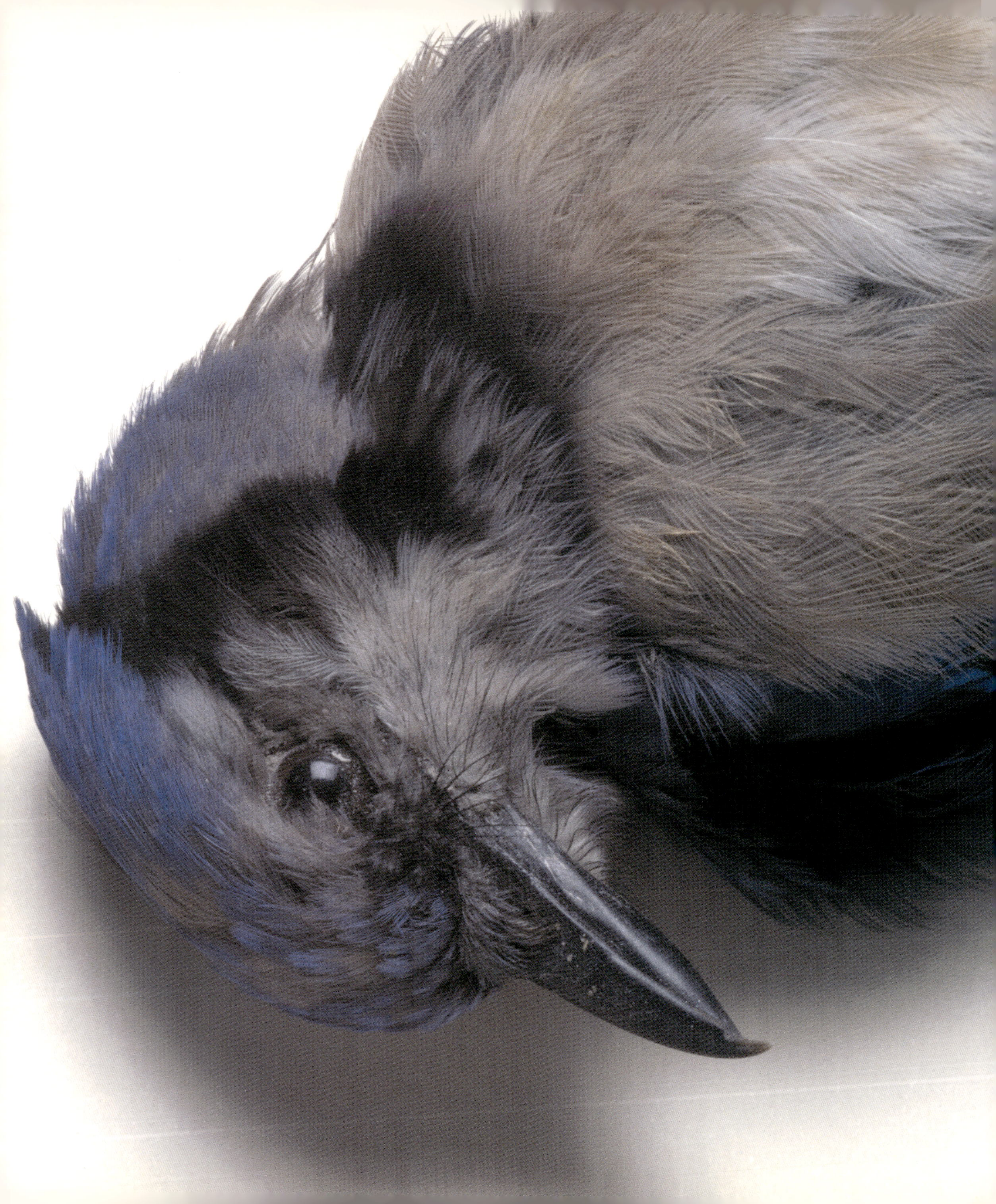

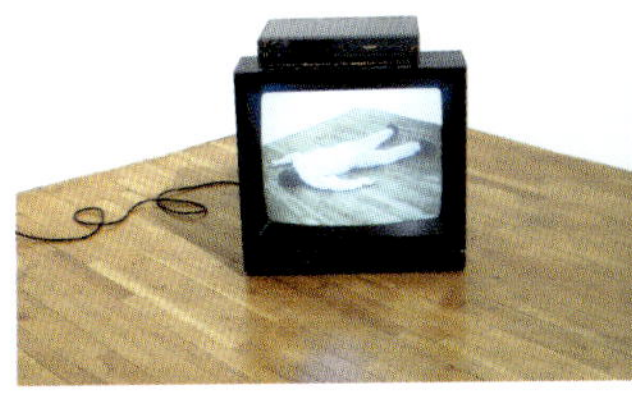

Listen closely to the carefully orchestrated soundtrack of Tony Tasset's **I Am U R Me**. Amid the scraping of spoons against cereal bowls and an occasional growl of a lawnmower, you will hear birds softly chirping outside— a beautiful nuance that could hardly be coincidental in such a biting moment of commercialized American perfection. One can't help but wonder if this cunning, cool conceptualist really has a soft spot for puppies, flowers and an occasional Michelle Pfieffer movie. But even if you buy that Tony actually does have Mr. Bluebird on his shoulder, works like **Dead Blue Jay** belie any overt sentimentality with a deep-seated memento mori theme.

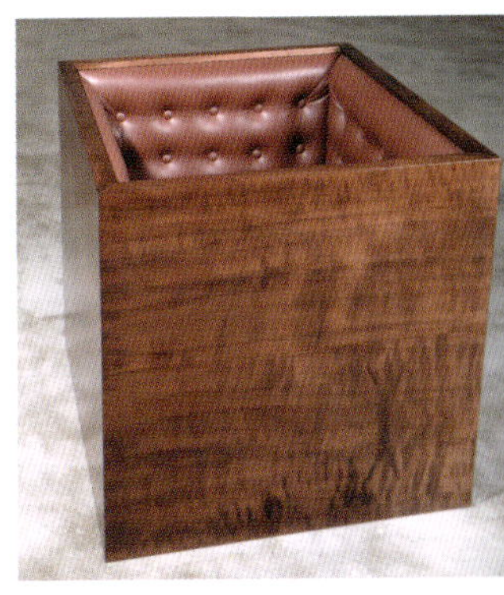

This is not the first of Tasset's works to deal with mortality. The **Domestic Abstraction** pieces, sporting various animal hides mounted and framed like hunters' trophies, embody a gruesome end in their genesis. The **Comfortable Abstraction** series featured slick, black-veneered "pedestals" with marble-headstone density, and belly-buttoned leather cushions which seemed to reference padded cells. Specifically, the sarcophagus-like **Sculpture Bench**, 1986, with its upholstered leather cushion and shallow plexiglass vitrine, clarifies that beneath the luster of spray-finished laquers and perfect mitres lies a sense of despair. Although "made" nearly fifteen years later, **Dead Blue Jay**, like a fine feathered Pope Julius, could easily complete this particular tomb-in-waiting.

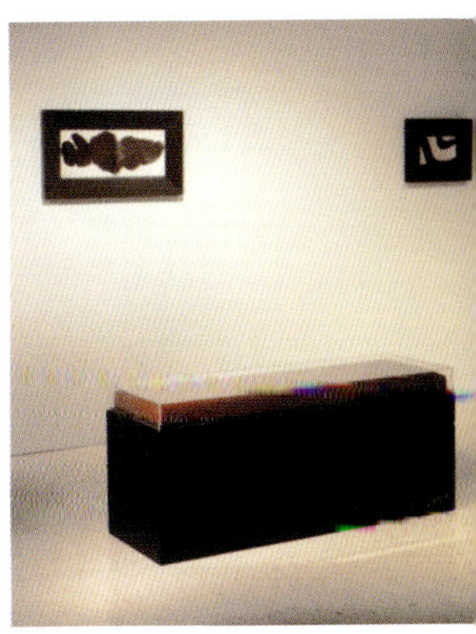

Tasset, Location Performance, 1993. Open Scultpure Bench, 1988. Installation view of *Anxious Objects* exhibition at University Galleries, 1987.
Opposite: Dead Blue Jay (detail), 2000.

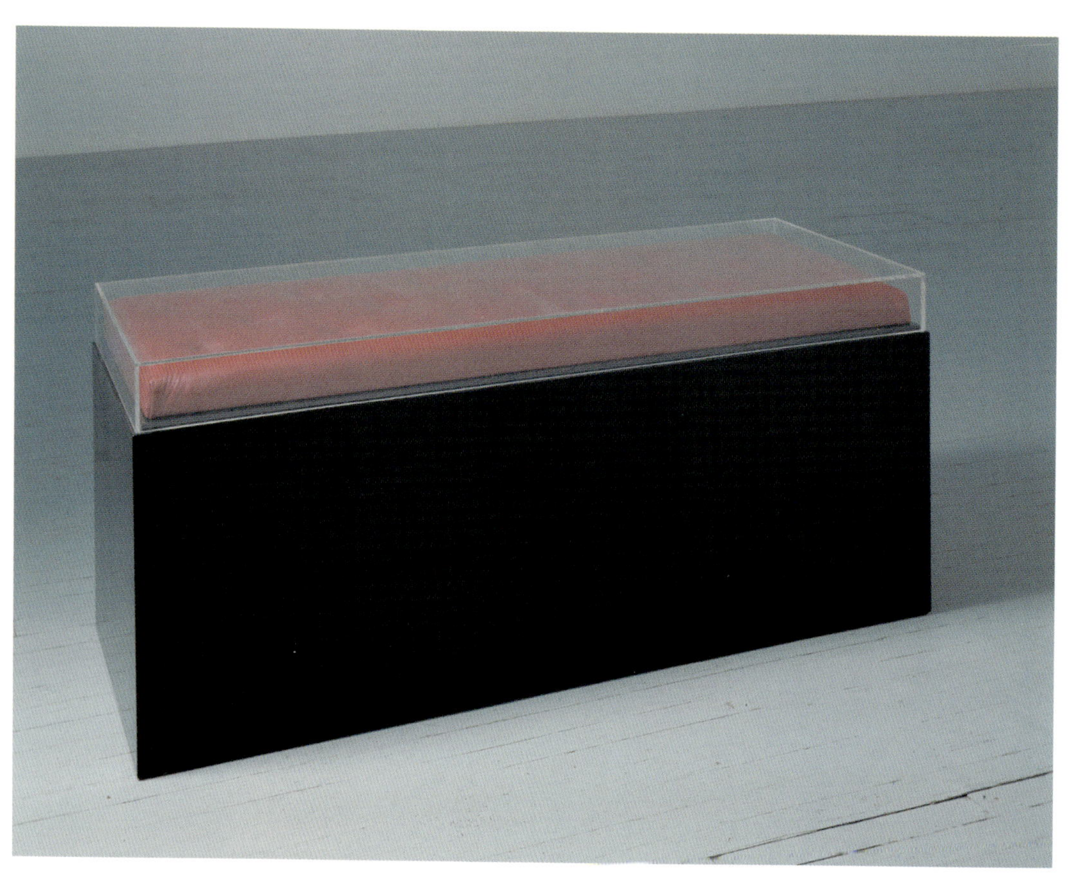

Sculpture Bench

Leather, plexiglass, and lacquered medite   22 x 19 x 55 inches   1986

Dead Blue Jay is displayed directly on the gallery floor, prompting a fortuitous discovery similar to the one its actual finder had. In the sky, perched in trees, roaming on the ground—birds are eerily everywhere, and much folklore and Hitchcock-inspired fear have traded on this fact. Birds are symbols of war and peace, omens of disaster, and predictors of plagues.

A symbolic scene at the end of David Lynch's *Blue Velvet* shows an obviously mechanical red-breasted robin gobbling a wasp. Its awkward simulacrum is mesmerizing and macabre. This scene, calling to mind Hitchcock's *The Birds*, prefigures in turn Tasset's subversive reverse-mimicry, Roni Horn's mummified owl portraits, and Gregory Crewdson's creature-filled suburban landscapes. Whether or not Tasset nods specifically to Lynch, his blue jay—a close relative to the crow and the raven—is a moody-blue presence of Poesque dimension, while its stiffened wings and tail recollect the meteoric velocity of Brancusi's *Bird in Space*.

Harnessing the bird's freedom by denying it a natural decomposition turns a subtle gesture of empathy and reverence into one of malevolence. A couple of weeks before his death, Barnett Newman stated that aesthetics to him must be what ornithology is to the birds. Relative to this particular fallen bird, can it also be said that Tasset's unfinished business with Modernism is alive and well?

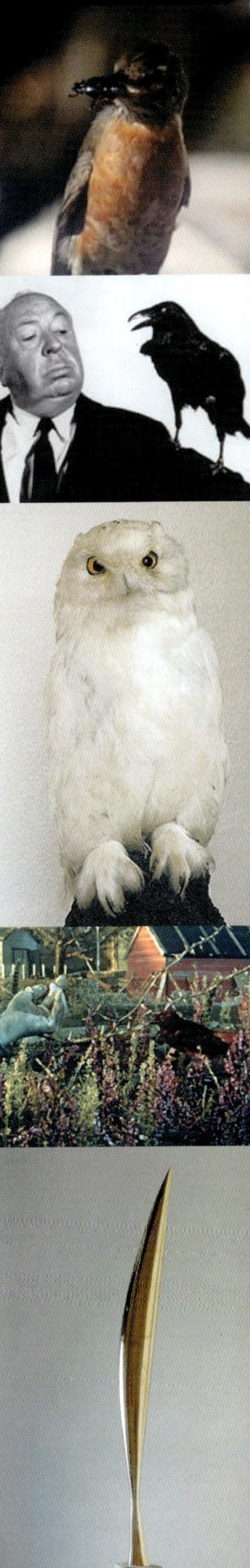

Top to bottom: Still from *Blue Velvet*, 1986. Alfred Hitchcock, promotional photo for *The Birds* Roni Horn, Dead Owl (detail), 1997. Gregory Crewdson, Untitled (detail), 1995. Constantin Brancusi, Bird in Space, 1928.

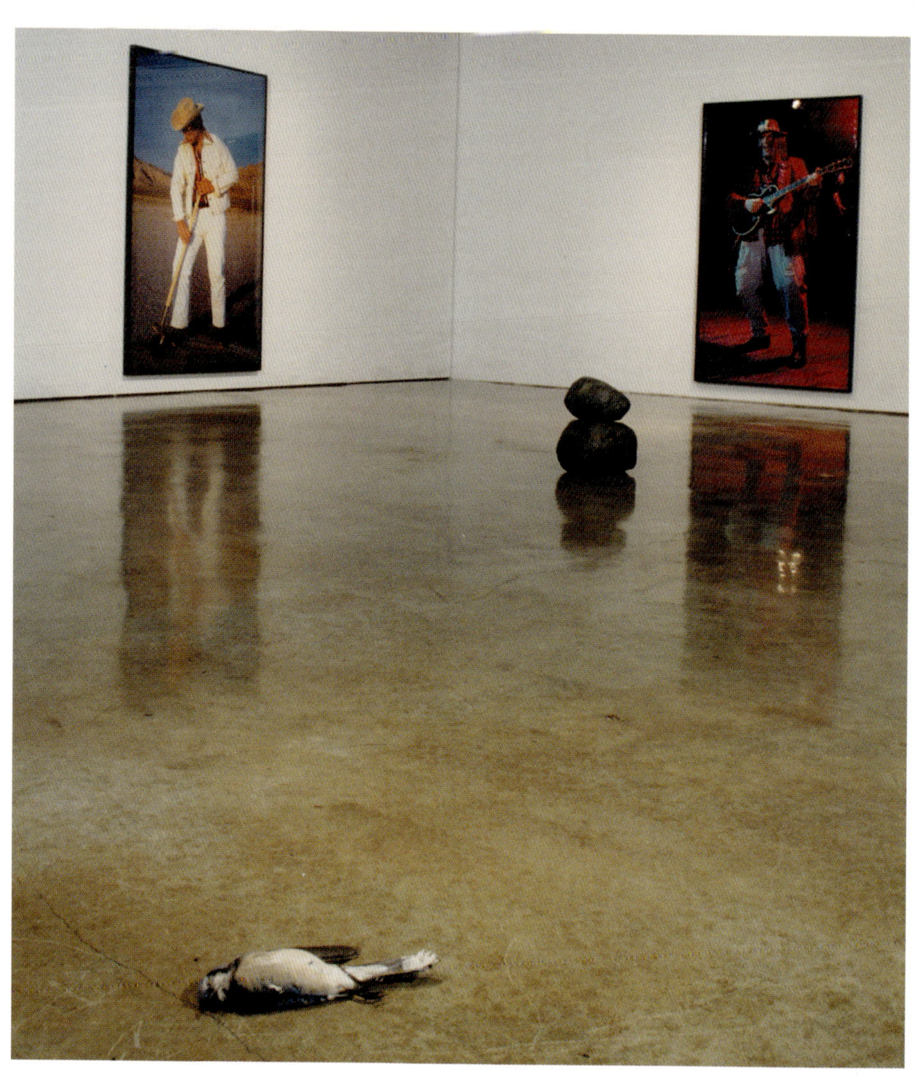

Installation view, University Galleries

Photo: Ted Diamond, 2003

Unless otherwise noted, all Tasset works in this monograph are courtesy Feigen Contemporary, New York. Height precedes width precedes depth, all measurements in inches.

Carving Again
DVD, :02 loop, no sound
2000

Cherry Tree
Oil paint, wax, steel armature, 120 x 144 x 144
1999

Dead Blue Jay
Taxidermied blue jay, 2 x 9 x 2.5
2000
Photo: Ted Diamond

The Eye
Cibachrome print, 48 x 60
2000

I Am U R Me
DVD, :30 loop with sound
1998

In My Room
DVD, 4:48, no sound
2000

I Peed in My Pants
Cibachrome print, 83.25 x 30.25
1994
Collection of Refco Group Ltd., Chicago

Judy Ledgerwood
Cibachrome print, 82 x 36
2000

Marker
Oil paint on Ultracal, 15 x 13 x 12
2000

My Garden
Cibachrome prints, 4 panels, 48 x 84 each
1993
Courtesy Christopher Grimes Gallery

My Parents
Cibachrome print, 52 x 72
1994

Neil Young
Cibachrome print, 82 x 48
1997

Robert Smithson
Cibachrome print, 83 x 49
1995
Photo: Oren Slor

Snowman
Polystyrene, fiberglass mesh, paper-mache, plaster, Sculpey, wax, steel, brass, acrylic beads, fake snow, acrylic and oil paint
71 x 55 x 40
2003
Photo: Ted Diamond

Spew
Black and white print, 48 x 48
1993
Courtesy Christopher Grimes Gallery, Santa Monica

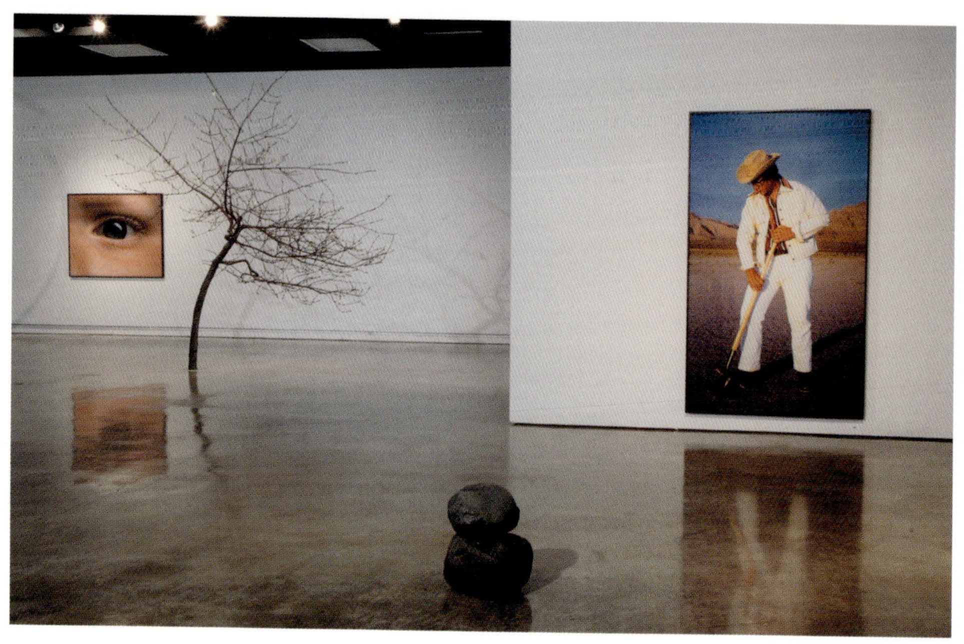

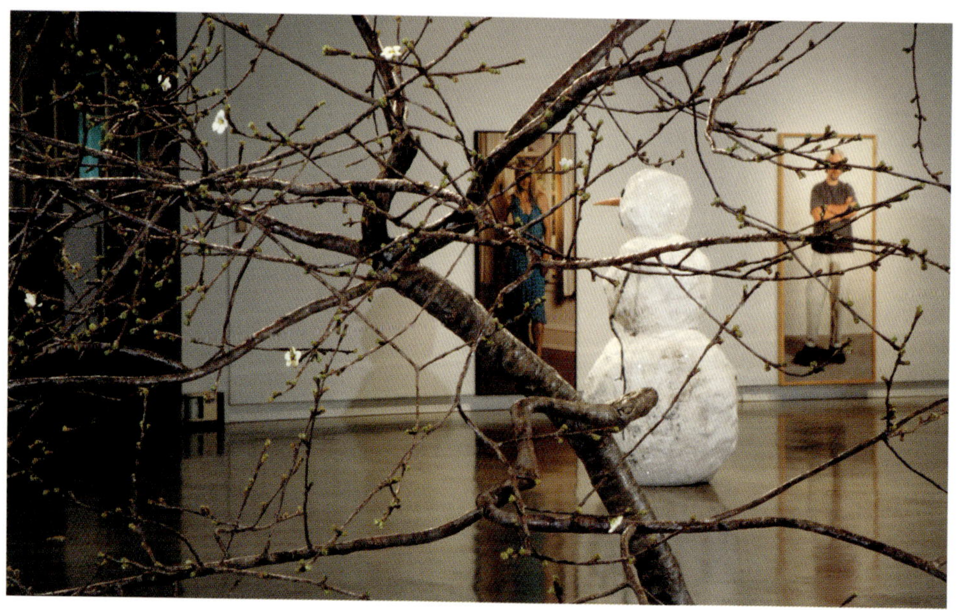

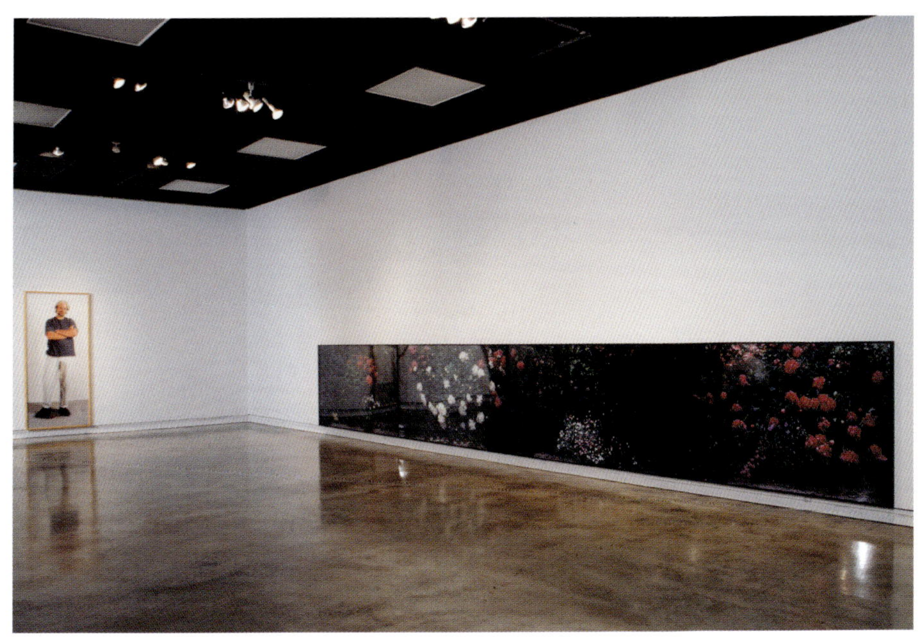

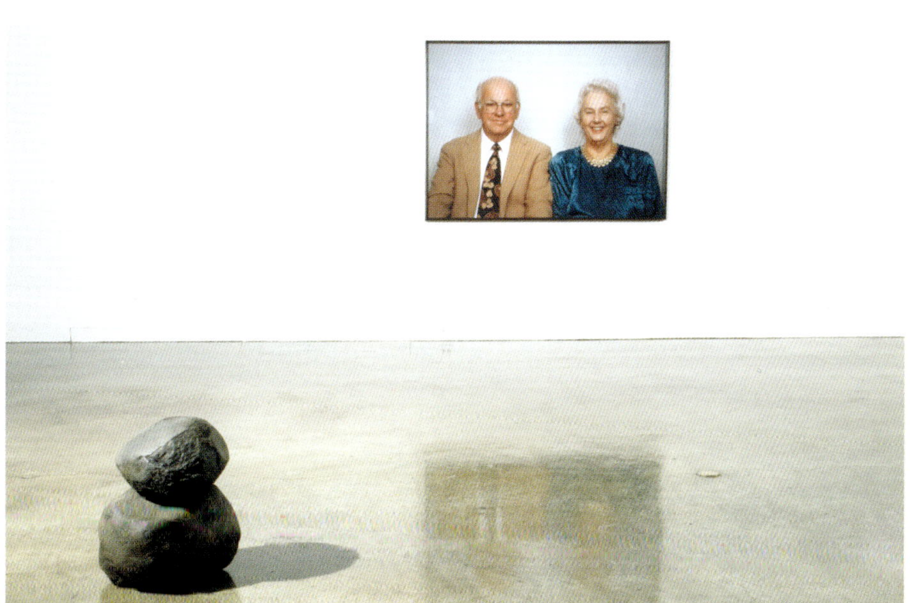

Installation views, University Galleries

Photos: Ted Diamond, 2003

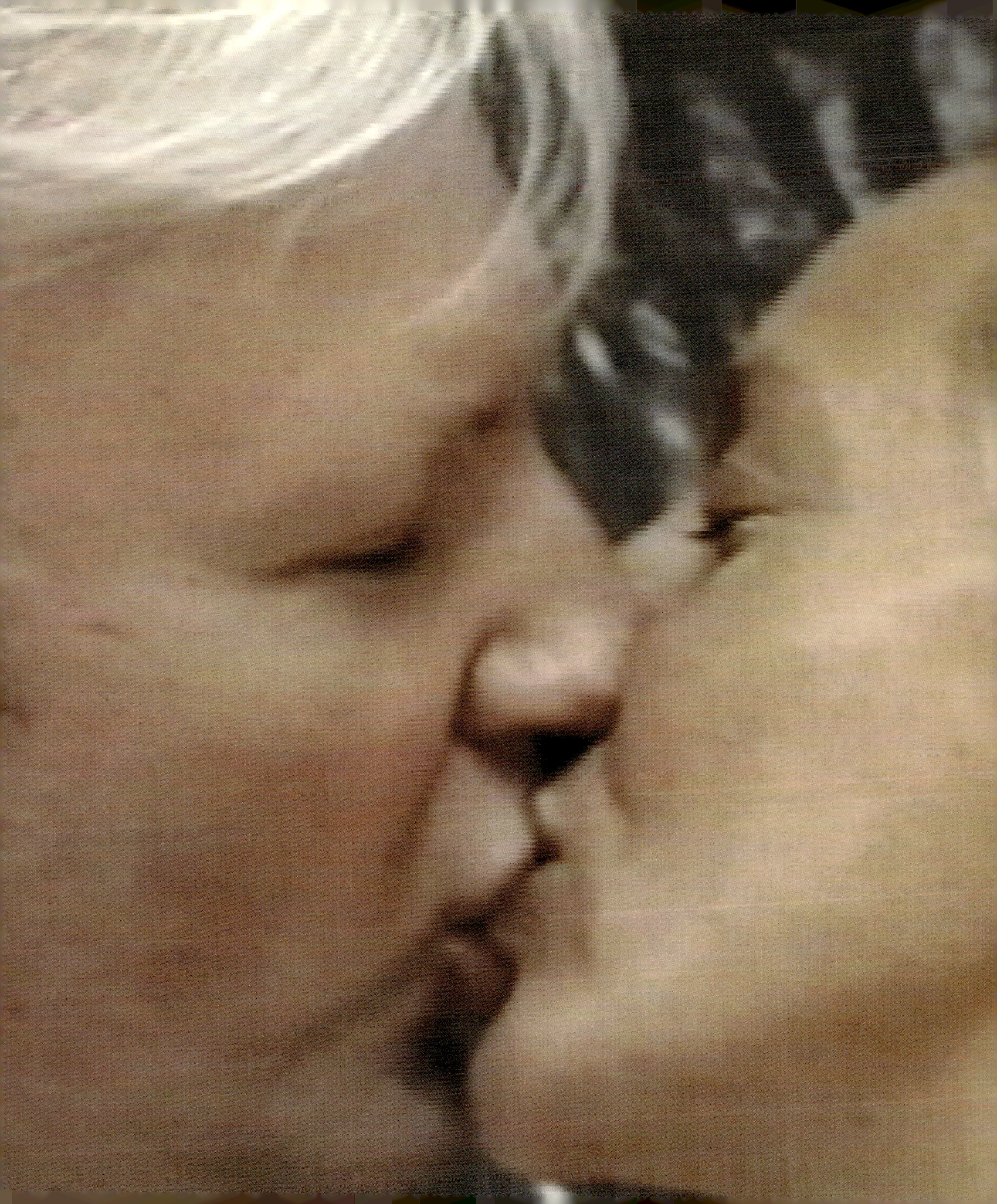

Born in Cincinnati, Ohio, 1960
Lives and works in Oak Park, Illinois

Education

1985	M.F.A., The School of the Art Institute of Chicago
1983	B.F.A., Painting, The Art Academy of Cincinnati
1983	Northwestern University, Evanston, IL

Teaching

1989 -	Professor, School of Art and Design, University of Illinois at Chicago

Solo Exhibitions

2003	University Galleries, Illinois State University, Normal, Illinois
	Portland Institute for Contemporary Art, Portland, Oregon
2002	Feigen Contemporary, New York
2001	*Judy*, Donald Young Gallery, Chicago
	Christopher Grimes Gallery, Santa Monica
2000	Feigen Contemporary, New York
	Tony Tasset: As it Is, The Contemporary Arts Center, Cincinnati
1998	*Tony Tasset*, Institute of Visual Arts, University of Wisconsin, Milwaukee
	Christopher Grimes Gallery, Santa Monica
1997	Feigen Contemporary, New York
	Christopher Grimes Gallery, Santa Monica
1996	Christopher Grimes Gallery, Santa Monica
	Manfred Baumgartner Gallery, Washington, D.C.
1995	Christopher Grimes Gallery, Santa Monica
	Robert Smithson/Tony Tasset: Site/Nonsite, Museum of Contemporary Art, Chicago (catalogue)
1994	Feature, New York
1993	Rhona Hoffman Gallery, Chicago
1992	Feature, New York
	Christopher Grimes Gallery, Santa Monica
	Galeria Pedro Oliveira, Porto, Portugal (catalogue)
	Shedhalle, Zurich, Switzerland (catalogue)
1991	Feature, New York
	Rhona Hoffman Gallery, Chicago
1990	Feature, New York
1989	Rhona Hoffman Gallery, Chicago
1988	Feature, New York
	Susanne Hilberry Gallery, Birmingham, Michigan
	Daniel Weinberg Gallery, Los Angeles
	Feature, Chicago
1987	Karsten Schubert, Ltd., London (catalogue)
1986	*Domesticates*, Feature, Chicago (brochure)
	Christine Burgin Gallery, New York

Selected Group Exhibitions

2003 *M_ARS. Art and War*, Neue Galerie am Landesmuseum Joanneum, Graz, Austria
lautoses irren/ways of woodworking 2, Staatsbank, Berlin, curated by Harm Lux
Life, Death, Love, Hate, Pleasure, Pain, Museum of Contemporary Art, Chicago
Chicago Artists in the New Millenium, Union League Club of Chicago

2002 *Kunst Nach Kunst*, Neuen Museum Weserberg, Bremen, Germany
Basics, Kunsthalle Bern, Bern, Switzerland (catalogue)
Looking At America, Yale University Art Gallery, New Haven, Connecticut
Individuality, Saks Fifth Avenue, New York
Sculpture in Chicago Now, Part II, Glass Curtain Gallery, Chicago, curated by Adam Brooks
Family, The Aldrich Museum of Contemporary Art, Ridgefield, Connecticut

2001 *Joy*, Ursula Blickle Stifung, Kraichtal, Germany
New Works, Feigen Contemporary, New York
At Home, Lennon, Weinberg, Inc., New York
Pictures, Patents, Monkeys, and More…On Collecting, Western Washington University, Bellingham;
John Michael Kohler Arts Center, Sheboygan, Wisconsin; Akron Art Museum, Akron, Ohio; Fuller
Museum of Art, Brockton, Massachusetts; Institute of Contemporary Art, University of Pennsylvania,
Philadelphia; Pittsburgh Center for the Arts, Pittsburgh; curated by Ingrid Schaffner

2000 *Life, after the Squirrel*, Location One, New York
Warning Shots, The Royal Armouries, Leeds, England
The Body in Photographs: A Recent Gift from Eileen and Peter Norton, Bard College, Center for
Curatorial Studies Museum, Annandale-on-Hudson, New York

1999-1998 *Mayday*, Centre d'Art Neuchâtel, Neuchâtal, Switzerland
minimal-MAXIMAL, Neues Museum Weserburg Bremen, Germany; Staatliche; Kunsthalle
Baden-Baden, Germany; Centro Galego de Arte Contemporanea, Santiago di Compostela,
Spain; National Museum of Contemporary Art, Seoul, Korea
Inglenook II, University Galleries, Normal, Illinois
Sweat, Camerawork, London
All of Me, New Langton Arts, San Francisco

1997 *ca-ca poo-poo*, Kolnischer Kunstverein, Cologne
Shot Reverse-Shot, Walter Phillips Gallery, Banff, Alberta, Canada, curated by Catherine Crowston

1996 *The Moral Imagination*, Plug-In Gallery, Winnipeg, California
Art in Chicago: 1945-1995, Museum of Contemporary Art, Chicago, curated by Lynne Warren (catalogue)
Persona, The Renaissance Society at the University of Chicago
Kunsthalle Basel, Basel, Switzerland; curated by Suzanne Ghez
Shit, Baron/Boisanté Gallery, New York, (poster)
Subverted Object, Ubu Gallery, New York
AbFab, Feature, New York

1995 *It's how you play the game*, Exit Art, New York, curated by Thelma Golden, Nancy Spector,
Robert Storr, Jeanette Ingberman and Papo Colo
Strung into the Apollonian Dream . . . An exhibition of a private collection, Feature, New York
Seven Longish Wooden Sculptures, Feature, New York
Art as Dramatic Comedy, Randolph Street Gallery, Chicago, curated by Marie Shurkus

1994 *The Ecstasy of Limits*, Gallery 400, School of Art and Design, The University of Illinois at
Chicago, curated by Yvette Brackman (catalogue)
Amenities, Frederick Layton Gallery, Milwaukee Institute of Art and Design, Milwaukee, curated by CAR

1993 *Mixed Messages: A Survey of Recent Chicago Art*, Forum for Contemporary Art, St. Louis,
curated by Christopher Scoates and Debra Wilbur
A Sequence of Forms: Sculpture by Illinois Artists, Chicago Cultural Center, Chicago, curated
by Edward M. Maldonado

| 1993 | *Mettlesome & Meddlesome: Selections from the Collection of Robert J. Shiffler*, Contemporary Arts Center, Cincinnati |

1993   *Mettlesome & Meddlesome: Selections from the Collection of Robert J. Shiffler*, Contemporary
Arts Center, Cincinnati

1992   *Paper Trails: The Eidetic Image*, Krannert Art Museum, University of Illinois at Urbana/Champaign;
I-Space, University of Illinois at U/C Gallery, Chicago, curated by Jerry Savage and Dan Socha
15th Anniversary Exhibition, Rhona Hoffman Gallery, Chicago
Editions: Functional Objects by Artists and Architects, Rhona Hoffman Gallery
Drawing New Conclusions, Betty Rymer Gallery, The School of the Art Institute of Chicago
Multiples, Randolph Street Gallery, Chicago

1991   *Office Party*, (March) Feature, New York
Galerie Anselmo Alvarez, Madrid, Spain, curated by Jane Gekler
Power: Its Icons, Myths and Structure in American Culture, 1961-1991, Indianapolis Art
Museum; Akron Art Museum, Akron, Ohio; Museum of Fine Art, Richmond, Virginia,
curated by Holliday T. Day (catalogue)
Stillstand Switches, Shedhalle, Zurich

1990   *Toward the Future Contemporary Art in Context*, Museum of Contemporary Art, Chicago (brochure)
Machine Shop, The Machine Shop at Emery, Cincinnati, curated by Derrick Woodham
Awards in the Visual Arts 9, New Orleans Museum of Art; Southeastern Center for
Contemporary Art, Winston-Salem, North Carolina; Arthur M Sackler Museum, Harvard
University, Cambridge; The BMW Gallery, New York (catalogue)
The Thing Itself, Feature, New York, (brochure)
Work on Paper, Paula Allen Gallery, New York
Outdoor Sculpture Show, Chicago Artists from Chicago Galleries, Klein Art Works, Chicago
New Generations Chicago, Carnegie Mellon Art Gallery, Carnegie Mellon University, Pittsburgh,
curated by Elaine A King (catalogue)
Oh, Those Four White Walls!: The Gallery as Context, Atlanta College of Art Gallery, curated by
Lisa Tuttle (catalogue)
Half-Truths, The Parrish Art Museum, Southampton, New York; curated by Marge Goldwater (catalogue)

1989   *Filling in the Gap*, Feigen, Inc., Chicago, curated by Saul Ostrow (catalogue)
FUNCTIONONFUNCTION, Suzan Rezac Gallery, Chicago (catalogue)
On Kawara: Date Paintings 1966-1988, The Renaissance Society at the University of Chicago
Signs of Life: Contemporary American Sculpture, Fundação Calouste Gulbenkian; Fundação Luso-
Americana Para O Desenvolvimento, Lisbon, Portugal, curated by Judith Russi Kirshner (catalogue)
Romancing the Stone, Feature, New York
Double Take, Contemporary Arts Center, Cincinnati, curated by Hudson
Reused, Althea Viafora Gallery, New York
Exhibition 12, Studio Arts Faculty, School of Art and Design, Gallery 400, University of Illinois at
Chicago (catalogue)
Dorothy, Center for Contemporary Art, Chicago, curated by Hudson

1988   *Walk Out to Winter*, Bess Cutler Gallery, New York, curated by Christian Leigh (catalogue)
Redefining the Object, University Art Galleries, Wright State University, Dayton, Ohio, and
Cleveland Center for Contemporary Art, Cleveland, Ohio, curated by Barry A. Rosenberg (catalogue)
Material Art, Althea Viafora Gallery, New York
John Baldessari: His Peers and His Persuasion, 1963-1988, Daniel Weinberg Gallery, Los Angeles,
and Leo Castelli Gallery, New York (catalogue)
Near Miss, Feature, Chicago
The Objects of Sculpture, The Arts Club of Chicago, curated by Neal Benezra (brochure)
Chicago Buy the Square Foot, Randolph Street Gallery, Chicago
Life Like, Lorence Monk Gallery, New York, curated by Marvin Heiferman
NYC #1/Sculpture, Rotterdam Arts Council, Rotterdam, The Netherlands; curated by Cees van der Geer
Information as Ornament, Suzan Rezac Gallery and Feature, Chicago (catalogue)
New York Now, Goteborgs Kunstmuseum; curated by Thord Thordeman, touring Sweden and Finland (catalogue)

1988	*Latitudes: Focus on Chicago*, The Aspen Art Museum, Aspen, CO (catalogue)
	Contemporary Icons and Explorations: The Goldstrom Family Collection, Davenport Museum of Art, Davenport, Iowa (catalogue)
1987	*The Non-Spiritual in Art Abstract Painting 1985-????*, 341 West Superior, Chicago, curated by Hudson (catalogue)
	Liars: A Question of Reason, State of Illinois Gallery, Chicago, curated by Debra Donato
	Nature, Feature, Chicago
	Anxious Objects, University Galleries, Illinois State University, Normal, Illinois; curated by Barry Blinderman (catalogue)
	(of Ever-Ever Land i speak), Stux Gallery, New York; curated by Christian Leigh (catalogue)
	Surfaces: Two Decades of Painting in Chicago, 1970s and 1980s, The Terra Museum, Chicago; curated by Judith Russi Kirshner (catalogue)
	A White Show, MoMing Gallery, Chicago; curated by Jeanne Dunning
	Postmodernism: A Spectacle of Reflexivity, UWM Art Museum, University of Wisconsin, Milwaukee, curated by Michelle Grabner (catalogue)
	A Different Corner: Definition and Redefinition, Painting in America, Biennal International de Pintura, U S Pavilion, Museo de Arte Moderne, Cuenca, Ecuador; curated by Christian Leigh (catalogue)
1986	*July*, Wolff Gallery, New York
	Larry Johnson, Tony Tasset, Christopher Wool, Kuhlenschmidt-Simon, Los Angeles
	One Hand Clapping, Karsten Schubert, Ltd, London
	Gilbert & George, Donald Judd, Tony Tasset, Christine Burgin Gallery, New York
	Industrial Icons, San Diego State University, San Diego
	Homer, Huttinger, Tasset, Feature, Chicago
	S.A.I.C.: A New Generation, Museum of Contemporary Art, Chicago, curated by Lynne Warren
	Painting and Sculpture Today, Indianapolis Museum of Art, Indianapolis (catalogue)
	Promises, Promises, Feature, Chicago and CAGE, Cincinnati; curated by Hudson
	Dull Edge, Randolph Street Gallery, Chicago, curated by Jeanne Dunning and Tony Tasset
1985	*Post Modern Conceptual Pop Production*, Feature, Chicago
	Two-person exhibition (with Mitchell Kane), School of the Art Institute of Chicago Gallery, Chicago
	Wilder Scholarship Retrospective, Chidlaw Gallery, Cincinnati
	Invitational, Feature and Rhona Hoffman Gallery, Chicago
	The Perfect Couple, CAGE, Cincinnati
1984	Two-person exhibition (with Greg Green), Bookspace, Chicago
	Sexuality in Art and the Media, School of the Art Institute of Chicago
1983	*Artists' Call*, Rhona Hoffman Gallery, Chicago

Public Commissions

| 2003 | Goldblatt's Building, Public Art Fund, Chicago |
| 2002 | Gateway Plaza, David L. Lawrence Convention Center, Pittsburgh (scheduled completion 2004) |

Collections

Art Institute of Chicago
Baltimore Museum of Art
Bard College Center for Curatorial Studies,
Annandale-on-Hudson, New York
Milwaukee Art Museum
Museum of Contemporary Art, Chicago
The Museum of Contemporary Art, Los Angeles
San Francisco Museum of Modern Art

Arning, Bill, review, *Time Out New York*, November 20-27, 1997, issue 113, p. 48

Artner, Alan, "Persona non grata," *Chicago Tribune*, March 17, 1996

__________ , "Sharp Conceptual Show Dares to be Different," *Chicago Tribune*, January 22, 1993, Section 7, p. 56

__________ , "Art in 3-D: Artists today do almost anything—except sculpt," *Chicago Tribune*, February 7, 1993, Arts, pp. 14-15

__________ , "Tasset's Works Activate Viewer's Participation," *Chicago Tribune*, January 13, 1989

__________ , "Tasset's Art Focuses on Presentation," *Chicago Tribune*, April 15, 1988, section 7, p.58

__________ , "Tony Tasset at Home with Clever Concept," *Chicago Tribune*, September 19, 1986, Section 7, p. 55

Barewaldt, Wayne, *The Plug in Harold*, Winnepeg, Ontario, October, 1996

Barnes, Lucinda, catalogue essay, "Robert Smithson/Tony Tasset: Site/Nonsite," Museum of Contemporary Art, Chicago , 1995

Blinderman, Barry, "On Art, Nature and Technology," catalogue essay for *Anxious Objects*, University Galleries, Illinois State University, Normal, IL, 1987

Bonesteel, Michael, "Medium Cool: New Chicago Abstraction," *Art in America*, December 1987, pp.138-147

Brown, Nate, "Art Appreciation," *Daily Vidette*, January 17, 2003, p. 11

Bulka, Michael, "Tony Tasset," *New Art Examiner*, March 1991, pp. 34-35

Campbell, Clayton, "The Visionary Landscape (review)," *Flash Art*, March/April 2000, p. 62

Cash, Stephanie, "Tony Tasset at Feigen Contemporary (review)," *Art in America*, March 1998, p. 101

Coburn, Marcia Froelk, "Minimalism to the Max," *Chicago Magazine*, October 13, 1993, pp. 94-99, 152

Colby, Joy Hakanson, "Lean Exhibit, Lots of Thought," *The Detroit News*, March 13, 1988, p. 3D

Cooke, Lynne, catalogue essay for exhibition at Karsten Schubert, Ltd., London, 1987

Curtis, Cathy, *Los Angeles Times*, July 22, 1988

Day, Holliday T, catalogue essay, *Painting and Sculpture Today*, Indianapolis Museum of Art, Indianapolis, 1986

Decter, Joshua, "New York in Review," *Arts*, Summer 1990, p. 96

Duffy, Robert W., "Getting the Message: Knowledge Distilled," St. Louis Post Dispatch, September 19, 1993, Section 3, p. 11

Dunning, Jeanne, catalogue essay, *Dull Edge*, Randolph Street Gallery, Chicago, 1986

Findsen, Owen, "'Banal' Burbs Turn Into Authentic Art," *The Cincinnati Enquirer*, April 2000

Frankel, David, "Tony Tasset, Feigen Contemporary," *Artforum*, February 2001, pp. 150-151

Gardner, Colin, review, *Los Angeles Times*, August 7, 1987, Part IV, p.16

Golden, Deven, review of "A White Show," *New Art Examiner*, March, 1987

Goldwater, Marge, catalogue essay, *Half-Truths*, The Parrish Art Museum, Southhampton, NY, 1990

Grabner, Michelle, "Hello Mr. Soul," (review), *Frieze*, Summer 1999, #47, p. 100

________________ , review, *New Art Examiner*, October, 1997, p. 50

________________ , catalogue essay, *A Spectacle of Reflexivity*, UWM Art Museum, University of Wisconsin, Milwaukee, 1986

Green, Ann Hunter, "Making the Art Rounds," *Where/Chicago*, September 1993, p. 26-27

Hapgood, Susan, "'Shit' at Baron/Boisanté," *Art in America*, March, 1997, pp. 109-110

Hawkins, Margaret, "It's a Girl Thing," *Chicago Sun-Times*, February 9, 2001, p. 46

Heartney, Eleanor, "Strong Debuts," *Contemporanea*, July/August 1988, p.110

Henry, Gerrit, "Tony Tasset at Christine Burgin (review)," *Art in America*, June 1987

Hixson, Kathryn, catalogue essay, *Tony Tasset:As It Is*, Feigen Contemporary, New York, 2000

______________ , "Transcendence to Transformation: The Art of Tony Tasset," *New Art Examiner*, May 2000, pp. 34-38

______________ , review, *FlashArt*, March/April, 1996, p. 114

______________ , *The Journal of Art*, February 1991, p. 68

______________ , "Chicago in Review," *Arts*, April 1991, p.106

______________ , "Cool, Conceptual, Controversial," *New Art Examiner*, May, 1988, pp. 30-33

Hudson, Kevin Maginnis and Richard Brettell, catalogue essays, *The Non-Spiritual in Art: Abstract Painting*, Chicago, 1986

Hugunin, James R., review, *New Art Examiner*, March 1989, p. 44

Holg, Garrett, "Sculptors Make Statements with Everyday Objects," *Chicago Sun-Times*, March 7, 1993, p. 13

Johnson, Ken, "Tony Tasset (review)," *New York Times*, October 31, 1997

J.Z., "Tony Tasset at Christopher Grimes," *d'Art International*, vol. 2, number 1, winter 1999.

Kandel, Susan, "Like Young," *Los Angeles Times*, May 29, 1997, p. 18.

Kertess, Klaus, catalogue essay, "Artschwager: His Peers and His Persuasion, 1963-1988," Daniel Weinberg Gallery, Los Angeles, CA and Leo Castelli Gallery, New York

King, Elaine A, catalogue essay, "New Generations: Chicago," University of Pittsburgh, Pittsburgh, 1990
Kirshner, Judith Russi, "The Benefit of the Doubt or Loving Modernism to Death," *Artforum*, November 1988, pp. 106-111
________________, catalogue essay, "Art in Chicago: 1945-1995," MCA Chicago
________________, catalogue essay, *On Kawara: Date Paintings 1966-1988*
________________, catalogue essay, *Surfaces: Two Decades of Painting in Chicago*, The Terra Museum, Chicago, 1986
Knight, Christopher, review, *Los Angeles Herald*, July 31, 1987
Knode, Marilu, "Tony Tasset," *Art/Text 61*, 1998, p. 48
Kutner, Janet, "Hybrid Film Mixes Facts, Fantasies," *The Dallas Morning News*, March 8, 1998.
Lambrecht, Luk (translated by Lynne George), "Olafur Gislason, Tony Tasset, Dieter Wymann" (review),
(Shedhalle), *Forum International*, May 1992, pp. 86-87
Lebovici, Elisabeth, "Liberation," *Guide*, October, 1996, p. 34
Leigh, Christian, catalogue essay, *Dorothy*, Center for Contemporary Art, Chicago, 1988
______________, "Summer Show (review)," *Artscribe International*, November/December, 1987
______________, catalogue essay, *A Different Corner: Definition and Redefiniton, Painting in America*, traveling exhibition, 1987
______________, catalogue essay, *of Ever-Ever Land I speak*, Stux Gallery, New York, 1986
Luecking, Stephen, review "New Works, Sequence of Forms," *Sculpture*, July-August 1993, pp. 57-58
Lippard, Lucy, catalogue essay, *Awards in the Visual Arts 9*, The BMW Gallery, New York, 1990
Mauro, Lucia, "Local artists hop on the cutting edge," *Pioneer Press*, February 1, 1995, B4-B5
McCormick, Carlo, catalogue essay, *New York Now*, Goteborgs Kunstmuseum, toured Sweden and Finland, 1988
McCracken, David, "Tasset Offers a Backstage Look at Slippery Sculptures," *Chicago Tribune*, January 11, 1991, Section 7, p. 8
______________, "Different Views of a Postmodernist World," *Chicago Tribune*, January 11, 1988, section 7 p. 60
Miles, Christopher, "Sharon Ellis and Tony Tasset," Artforum.com, 2002, on website
Miro, Marsha, "Frames Tame Wild Things," *Detroit Free Press*, March 24, 1988, p. 5C
Moody, Tom, review, *Art Papers*, November/December, 1996, p. 56
Morgan, Robert, "New York in Review," *Arts*, February 1989, p. 98
Nagy, Peter, "Shit (review)," *Time Out*, Oct. 31-Nov. 7, 1996, Issue #58, p. 48
New Yorker, April 29, 1991, p. 17
Noll, Damien, "Pixels and Particles, Pigment and Stone," *Chicago Journal*, February 2001, p. 9
Ostrow, Saul, catalogue essay, *Filling in the Gap*, Feigen, Inc, Chicago, 1989
Paine, Janice T., "Amenities: A strangely discomforting exhibit," *Milwaukee Sentinel*, October 14, 1994, 8E
Pinto De Almeida, Bernardo, "Tony Tasset" (catalogue essay), from exhibition at Galeria Pedro Oliveira, Portugal, 1992
Robinson, Walter, "Weekend Update," artnet.com>reviews, October 25, 2000.
______________, "State of the Art: Young, Gifted and Affordable," *Metropolitan Home*, November 1987, pp. 58-59
Rosenberg, Barry A, catalogue essay, *Redefining the Object*, University Art Galleries, Wright State University, Dayton Ohio
   and Cleveland Center for Contemporary Art, Cleveland, Ohio, 1988
Runólfsson, Halldór Björn, catalogue essay, *Stillstand Switches*, Shedhalle, Zurich, Switzerland, 1992
Scanlan, Joe, "Money-Market," *dialogue*, January 1987, p. 26.
Schaffner, Ingrid and Therese Cafaro, catalogue essays, *Shit*, Baron Boisante Gallery, New York
Schjeldahl, Peter, "At the Salon of April," *Village Voice*, May 14, 1991, p. 86
Schultz, Jerome, "Postmodernism, A Spectacle of Reflexivity (review)," *New Art Examiner*, June 1987, p. 55
Sherlock, Maureen P, "Tony Tasset," *Arts*, Summer 1989, p. 82
Snodgrass, Susan, "Tony Tasset at Rhona Hoffman (review)," *Art in America*, January, 1994, pp. 110-111
Sobel, Dean, catalogue essay, *Identity and Recent Self-Portraiture*, 1997, Milwaukee Art Museum
Stevens, Mitchell, "Forms to Warm the Heart," *Reader*, February 19, 1993, p. 29
"Sunday Style," *The New York Times*, February 25, 2001.
Tasset, Tony, catalogue essay, *Domesticates*, Feature, Chicago, 1986
__________, "The Beast is Now Under Control," *Nit & Wit*, October 1986, p. 15
Taylor, Sue, review of *Liars*, *Art in America*, September 1987, pp. 187, 189
Waddington, Christopher, *Contemporary Icons and Explorations: The Goldstrom Family Collection*, Davenport Museum of Art,
Davenport, Iowa, 1988

Wainwright, Martin, "Warning Shots: Royal Armouries Exhibits Art of Violence," *The Guardian,* May 13, 2000.

Walker, Hamza, "Eureka! I've Lost It," catalogue essay, *Persona,* 1996.

Walker, Hamza and Susan Stryker, catalogue essays, *Kunsthalle Basel,* Basel, Switzerland

Warren, Lynne, catalogue essay, *S.A.I.C.: A New Generation,* Museum of Contemporary Art, Chicago, 1986

Wehr, Anne, "Tony Tasset," *Time Out New York,* November 23-30, 2000

Wilk, Deborah, "Robert Smithson, Tony Tasset (review)," *New Art Examiner,* January, 1996

______________, "The Ecstasy of Limits (review)," *New Art Examiner,* February, 1995, p. 38

Yood, James, catalogue essay, *The Refco Collection,* Sue Taylor, editor, The Refco Group, Ltd, Chicago,1990, pp. 178-79

______________, catalogue essay, *Exhibition 12,* Studio Arts Faculty, School of Art & Design, University of Illinois at Chicago, Gallery 400, Chicago, 1988

Yood, James, "Tony Tasset (review),"*Artforum,* March 1991, p. 134

"What's Happening in New York," *Atelier, Magazine of International Art,* April, 1994, p. 45

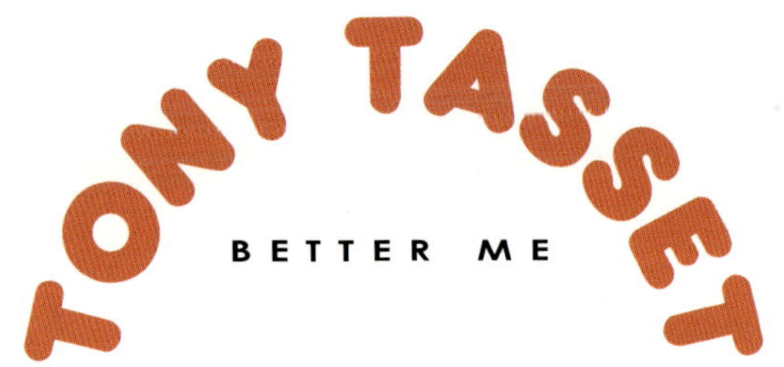

We would like to thank the following for their help in making this exhibition and catalogue possible: Angela Barker, Robert Clark, Feigen Contemporary, Ben Gardner, Michelle Grabner, Christopher Grimes, Stuart Horodner, Hudson, Robin Hulesbus, the Illinois Arts Council, Lance Kinz, Dave Kuntz, Judy Ledgerwood, Shona MacDonald, Martin Patrick, Elizabeth Randall, Refco Group Ltd., Susan Reynolds, Shawn Smith, and Stanley So.

ILLINOIS STATE
UNIVERSITY

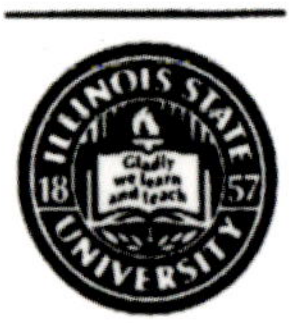